Get Up and Grow

Get Up and Grow

How to Motivate Yourself and Everyone Else Too

Philippa Davies

Hodder & Stoughton

First published in Great Britain in 2001 by Hodder and Stoughton
A division of Hodder Headline

A CIP catalogue record for this title
is available from the British Library.

ISBN 0 340 79444 5

Typeset by Phoenix Typesetting, Ilkley, West Yorkshire
Printed and bound in Great Britain by Clays Ltd, St Ives plc

Hodder and Stoughton
A division of Hodder Headline
338 Euston Road
London NW1 3BH

For Betty Davies, mother-in-law from Heaven.

Contents

Acknowledgements

Thanks to Rowena Webb, Rosemary Trapnell and everyone else at Hodder who works on behalf of my books. Thanks, too, to Vicki McIvor and to my family and friends. Special thanks to Tim Shore, for creating the name *getupandgrow*.

Part 1

Motivating Yourself

1 *The Big Impetus*

A couple of years ago I went to a talk by an eminent professor of child psychology. At the end of his talk, he described his feelings about bringing up his own children.

'There is one really big regret I have,' he said, 'and that is that I did not bring my children up to be entrepreneurial; I did not concentrate on developing their self-sufficiency and motivational abilities.' The middle-class audience shifted rather uncomfortably. We were all bringing up our little Emmas and Charlies to do well at school and to become surgeons and lawyers. We weren't rearing them to cope with disappointment, difficult people and the several different directions their lives were likely to take. We made mental notes to change emphasis.

It is this change in emphasis that this book is all about. Whatever you are doing in life today – building a career, starting your own business, bringing up children – it needs to be done entrepreneurially. And to live entrepreneurially we must be confident of our ability to motivate ourselves and others. It is this ability that will be at the heart of everything we do.

Our get up and grow world

There have been profound changes in our culture and workplace over the past twenty years or so. Institutionalised authority in the form of the church, government and the royals has lost its power and appeal, and individualism now prevails. Morality and gender roles have become blurred, while traditional families are in decline. In general terms, speed and flexibility are paramount in the work-place, and there is little long-term job security. We now rely on ourselves rather than on strong leadership; we invent our own jobs rather than having them handed to us on a plate.

Now this may make some of you shudder, but there is a huge upside to all of this. We have far more choice in how we live our lives. If our relationships don't work out, then we need no longer hang on in there for fear of the wrath of the parish elders. The speed of change and flexi-bility required means that we don't need to worry about making the wrong career decision at twenty-one, and then being stuck with it in a 'nine-to-five sort of quiet desper-ation' for our entire lives. If we wish, and provided we make wise choices along the way, we can change direc-tion, live and work in all sorts of different ways, and have serial professions – provided we wish to do these things. We can seize opportunities more frequently and reinvent ourselves periodically.

But this constantly changing environment also means that we have to be exceptionally well-equipped to deal with unpredictability. We have to be able to motivate ourselves and others in the face of the unexpected. We get a new and awkward boss, we lose a contract, our child's confidence gets knocked at school: these are everyday situations that most of us face in our turbulent world. Now, more than ever, we need the resources to pick ourselves up, dust ourselves down and resume battle. Resilience and self-reliance are the order of the day. And that is why I've written this book.

Even those of us in relatively stable workplaces will find that the demands of our roles have changed. Command and control organisations have become focused on coaching and commitment. The other day, a friend who runs training for a large retail company was telling me about the concerns of managers in his organisation. 'Tell me what to do,' they say to him, 'I was trained to become a manager who controlled people and now I'm supposed to motivate them. How on earth do I do that?' And that's another reason why I've written this book. It's for people who feel they need new people skills, which they were never taught.

Finally, I wrote the book because of something that happened to me. No need to cue the melancholic violin strings quite yet – it's just that this incident really seemed to illustrate to me the sort of world we inhabit. About a year and a half ago, my work was really exciting. I started a week one Monday morning with two likely television series looming and a publishing deal to write a series of about eighteen books. By Friday, I knew I was not wanted for either series, and the deal to write the eighteen books – one of which I'd already written – had collapsed. The publishing company was up for sale. It was obviously not a good week for those of us born under Aries. Some wine and whinging later, I picked myself up and work has got really exciting again. That week really made me think about how quickly our fortunes can change, and how we need to develop resilience to deal with this.

Macho motivation

Like most writers, when I get the germ of an idea I usually look at what else has been written on the subject. On the whole, motivation has been treated as a pretty macho subject: you know the sort of book, with a sharp salesman in a shiny suit on the cover. However, as a mum it struck me that the workings of motivation are important in so many contexts: getting back to work after a career break, starting your own business, and motivating partners, friends and children who need a boost. And there are also those more obvious aims of improving performance – our own and other people's – and success at work. In fact, in any sort of change or self-improvement – diet, exercise or being nicer to your mother-in-law – motivation matters.

Our ability to motivate ourselves and others affects our relationships, too. If you're anything like me, you will have times where you just have to avoid your 'downer' friends – those people who frequently lack motivation and campaign to demotivate everyone else as well. Then there are others who you can always rely on for encouragement and inspiration – people you want to spend time with, no matter how you are feeling, and whose invites to lunch always lift your spirits.

Meaningful motivation

Our beliefs about other people are often created by how we interpret their motivation; for instance: 'all men are selfish' or 'all women are after one thing – money'. In west Wales where I grew up, the view was often expressed that 'It's the English who come down here to make money'. I grew up with the impression that all English people were clever, good at business and motivated largely by profit. When I went to university in England, I discovered this was not the case. But because beliefs put powerful filters onto how we perceive the world, if we believe a person to be motivated strongly by an urge (say greed), we will jolly well see evidence of that greed in much of what they do. Wiser, probably, to remember that human beings are very complex.

But that hasn't stopped experts from trying to explain human motivation in a categorical and definitive way. Freud, based on studies of his own distressed patients, concluded that much of our motivation was unconscious. We act on deep and hidden motives to do with sex, aggression and anxiety. Like me, you may find it wiser to avoid a Freudian approach when you're having a bad day.

In contrast, Maslow, often referred to in business psychology, studied highly effective individuals like Eleanor Roosevelt, Abraham Lincoln and Albert Einstein. He described a hierarchy of needs starting with our most basic needs for survival and rising to the ultimate need, which was for 'self-actualisation'. Jung and Carl Rogers also shared this optimistic view, that we are driven to realise our full potential, in creative and spiritual ways. This view has become the backbone of the self-help culture of America.

From his work with children, Piaget described three phases of motivation: the first where they wanted to conform, to learn the rules of the game; the second, where they realised that the rules of the game could be changed, and the third stage, where they realised that they could feel empathy. Yes, it may be occurring to you that you know some adults who never reached that third stage.

Finally and so that you get a rounded view of the expertise, I should mention another influential school: behaviourism. Hull, a behaviourist, emphasised how we were motivated by needs for survival and to reduce tension; therefore, we behave in a particular way to ensure that we and our offspring will thrive, and when something we want is difficult to get, we act to close that gap.

Like many others, my view is that we are very complex as human beings, and useful as it would be to have one single explanation of what motivates us, it would be wishful thinking.

The get up and grow story

I work as an organisational psychologist, which means much of the time I help people communicate better at work. Very often this communication has the purpose of motivating people. Sometimes I work on especially interesting motivational missions: in the 1997 election campaign I advised Labour Party campaign organisers on how to motivate volunteers and campaign workers, while in the 2001 campaign I advised cabinet ministers.

Now you might expect me to be a relentlessly cheerful positive thinker, but I'm not. I'm quite optimistic on the whole, but I like my share of dark ruminations, too. And during the writing of this book I've had opportunities to do just that, as early on in its preparation my partner was taken seriously ill with myocarditis, a virus that attacks the heart. His recovery has involved a great deal of rest. We have two small boys, so quite often starting on my book on Monday mornings I would be feeling – in a word – knackered. But however exhausting, this experience has provided great field study for the book. Rather than brightly breezing through it, I've really had to apply the ideas about which I'm writing to the book's creation. Most usefully, I've kept relatively cool, broken the work down into small chunks, maintained a sense of humour, gone to the gym erratically and drunk lots and lots of cups of tea.

Having the mother-in-law from heaven has helped, too.

Well, bully for you, you may be thinking. What about us, your readers? You may be reading this as someone who has had a great deal of tragedy in their lives, or someone who is just interested in self-development and likes occasionally to read books on the subject. Either way, there should be something for you here, as I've aimed to keep the context fairly broad. This is self-help for real life, so the book is full of practical tips and ideas that you can use immediately. There are also lots of stories to which I hope you will be able to relate. I aim to inspire you to look at your life, work and family slightly differently, as areas loaded with potential for you to practise your marvellous motivational powers.

It's rather a cliché to say about life that 'This is the real thing, not a dress rehearsal', but a lot of people live dress rehearsals, simply because they cannot motivate themselves to achieve their dreams and ambitions. This book will teach you all you need to know to motivate yourself – and others – to create the happiness and fulfilment that can be achieved when we live life not as a dress rehearsal, but as a dazzling Broadway run.

If you enjoy the book and would like to take your interest further, then do use my contact details at the back to find out about workshops.

Goodies within

I wanted to write a book that was not just for corporate warriors, but for those of us who try to be corporate amazons, caring professionals, good mums and dads, and friends and lovers, too. These days, we are much less likely to admire people who are nakedly self-seeking. We realise that the great art in being human is to strike a balance between looking after ourselves and connecting to and helping others – in other words, acting on 'enlightened self-interest', as writer Dorothy Rowe calls it. But, of course, you can't motivate other people unless you understand how to motivate yourself. That's why there are two sections in this book. This first seven chapters are all about self-motivation, while the last chapters focus on motivating others.

I have studied people with differing amounts and types of motivation, and their prime attribute seemed to be how they handled their moods. Some of them showed great ability to be able to control how they were feeling, and to disguise it when necessary. Others would wake up in the morning in the grips of a low mood, and be unable to shake it off throughout the day, remaining completely demotivated. For that reason, this book will focus on moods, how they affect our motivation, and how we can use them to our advantage.

The trouble is that, however good we are at controlling our moods, we sometime encounter a human bollard. That is, someone who is just downright difficult and awkward, and no amount of happy thinking on our behalf can do anything about them. It's equally important to learn how to deal with 'downer' people as it is to learn to cope with these feelings in ourselves. We'll look at just what needs to be done to keep the ball rolling.

Feeling motivated is also very much about using our creativity. This is a word that causes people all sorts of problems – you know, the art master may have told us we didn't have any, or we regard it as a word synonymous with disorder and chaos. My view is that creativity should be far more central role in how we live, work and learn together, and here you'll find ways to access and develop the creativity that every one of us undoubtedly shares.

Modern life is littered with pitfalls and minefields, and no matter how motivated we may be at the outset, there are always times when we are caught unawares and find it difficult to keep things going. A proportion of this book is devoted to keeping ourselves motivated through change and coping with a variety of different crises. This will include the sort of change where we have to go it alone through leaving relationships or employment, for instance. If you need motivation to find motivation, it's all here.

It's fairly obvious and accepted knowledge that women and men's brains are wired differently, so it seems sensible that they might be motivated in quite different ways in certain situations. We'll look at what approaches suit each sex best. We'll also look at how we motivate others at work, and how we can use the best behaviour signals and words to help us with this task. Finally, we'll look at motivating family and friends, with ideas about how to motivate a demoralised partner or child, and how to boost a needy friend.

Get growing *now*

It would be wonderful if there was one single simple key to motivation, but there ain't. Indeed, if writing this book has done anything, it's reaffirmed one of the few certainties I hold: that people are very complicated. There's no one strategy or theory that will apply to everyone, so I've provided lots of ideas and tips so that you can find the one that works best for you and try it out.

One of the ultimate aims of this book is to help you to understand yourself and other people a bit better. It will bring you closer to achieving your ambitions and dreams. It will show you that there are hundreds of ways to motivate yourself more effectively.

How exciting! You're not looking backwards, you're not standing still, you're going to get out there and get up and grow. My website, which shares a title with this book, occasionally has hits from people looking for horticultural advice. They want to know how to make their seedlings grow. Despite the mistake, I'd like to think they still find the content nurturing and sustaining. I hope you experience this book in the same way. Enjoy my fertiliser.

2 *Mood Magic*

'Consistency is contrary to nature, contrary to life.'
Aldous Huxley

I recently joined a creative writing class where we're given writing tasks to do in between the weekly meetings. Every week, one or two members of the group haven't been able to write anything, and the most common excuse is: 'I just couldn't get in the mood.' I suspect that what they mean is that their state of mind prevented them from mustering self-belief. Those of us who write as a job, or as a habit, are rarely affected by mood; deadline pressures see to that. We just plonk ourselves down in front of the screen and hey, diddle, diddle, off we go.

Now, I don't want to sound unsympathetic, but I think that being affected by our moods to the extent that they prevent us from getting motivated means that it's worth trying to understand just what moods are, and how we can control them. Rather than feeling controlled and de-motivated through our moods, we can, when we know a bit more about them, stand back, assess what's going on, and do something constructive about it. We can perform mood magic on ourselves.

So why do moods demotivate us? Well, our predictions regarding what we can or can't do usually depend on our current state of mind. Let's say that on the whole you regard yourself as a pretty positive person, but are experiencing an unusually melancholic mood. A friend asks you to join them on a ten-mile sponsored walk. You balk at the idea and decline, even though you'd normally relish it as a challenge. The next day, when the melancholy has passed, you phone your friend and explain that you've changed your mind. Your mood was the main factor in your original decision, even though it was an unusual state for you and unrepresentative of how you are most of the time.

In psychological literature, the subject of motivation almost always includes mention of Albert Bandura's theory of 'self-efficacy'. Bandura found that the extent to which people believed themselves to be effective was very significant in terms of what they achieved. Furthermore – surprise, surprise – we are far more likely to be successful at something when we believe ourselves to have self-efficacy, or, in other words, to be effective. When our mood is low, we are unlikely to regard ourselves as being effective.

Linked to this is a psychological theory I have invented, which is called the 'ensurance theory' and it is a theory of 'self-inadequacy'. It goes like this: if we believe we're not good enough to do something, we will jolly well ensure that we fail at it, because that makes us right. And for some of us, being right is more important than succeeding.

Some of us may have horrible memories of this theory at work when we recall our exams. We dreaded an exam and thought we are going to fail, so to ensure that this happened, we left little time to revise. Hooray, then, when our poor results proved us right. This type of behaviour is practised all the time – when we have tight deadlines, reports to write or even a job interview for which to prepare. We set up failure when we feel inadequate because we'd rather be proved right than be seen to fail.

How moods work

A mood is a state of being that is milder than an emotion and we usually experience it over a longer period of time.

It will be created and affected by biochemical factors, such as blood sugar levels, hormones, low energy levels, lack of sleep, and also psychological factors, such as how we perceive and react to things that happen to us. Our positive moods tend to be more influenced by whether we *feel* good or not; our negative moods tend to be more influenced by bad events that happen to us. For example, you may be in an upbeat mood when you are told that a project you've been looking forward to at work has been postponed . . . and still remain pretty upbeat. On the other hand, if you receive the same news in a bleak mood, that mood is likely to be exacerbated.

Our moods have four main characteristics: how energetic we feel, contrasted with how tired we feel; how calm we feel, contrasted with how tense we feel. So we can draw a mood map of the possibilities:

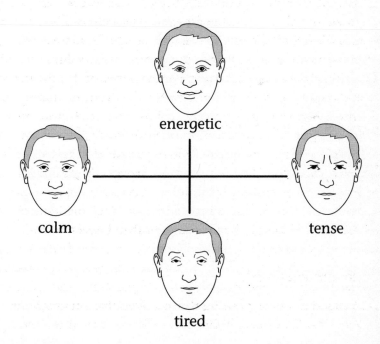

energetic

calm

tense

tired

A lot of the time we do things to regulate our moods without perhaps being fully aware of this intention. For many of us, late afternoon is a vulnerable time for experiencing a mood of tense tiredness; and that's when we tend to grab the biscuit or the strong espresso to keep us going through till evening and make us feel better.

Wired, weary, poised and pacified

These are the most common moods people experience and the more we know about them, the more we can do something to prevent them from acting as demotivators:

Wired. This is a tense and energised state, where you feel ready for action but also wound-up. Wired is what a lot of us feel when the train service has prevented us from being on time for a meeting, and we have drunk lots of coffee as a means of distraction.

Weary. This is a tense and tired state, where you feel exhausted but also prickly and hyper-sensitive to provocation. PMS calling here for some of us, perhaps. This state is familiar to people who are working hard at a time when they really feel ready for a break, and are battling on through the tiredness, with or without the help of boosters like cigarettes, caffeine and sugar.

Poised. This is a calm state but one where you feel energetic, too. You are ready for action, and a good balance encourages a sense of self-possession. This is a great mood to be in – good for our health and for other people around you. The more you put yourself in situations where you experience this mood, the more motivated you will feel.

Pacified. This is a calm but tired state – the kind that mothers love to see babies drifting into at four o'clock in the morning. This state is actually quite pleasant – the sort of feeling we get when we've really worked hard and well, and following a fine glass of Burgundy we drift off into a sweet sleep.

Two other labels we tend to stick on our moods are the words 'depressed' and 'anxious'.

Depression. This is a low energy state, where our nervous systems are under-aroused and we feel like we can do very little. The word 'depressed' covers a wide variety of states: from mild blues to a severe clinical disorder. Reactive depression is related to events such as bereavement, loss of health, divorce or redundancy. Endogenous depression happens suddenly and without any apparent explanation, and it can recur. How do you know whether 'the blues' are in fact depression? Well, if you've been feeling down for more than two months, you should visit your doctor.

Anxiety. In contrast, this is a high-energy state, where there is a gap between what we think is happening and what makes us feel safe We will feel agitated until we perceive that we can close this gap and busy ourselves with action to cope with this.

Both anxiety and depression may be caused by biochemical or emotional problems, and, indeed, many people suffer from both. Identifying whether our mood is characterised by the tense energy of anxiety or the lower energy of depression can help us to deal with it more effectively.

Mood-mapping

Typically over a day, our energy levels rise to a peak just before or after lunch, drop off to a low late afternoon, and then rise again mid-evening, dropping off towards midnight. Something like this:

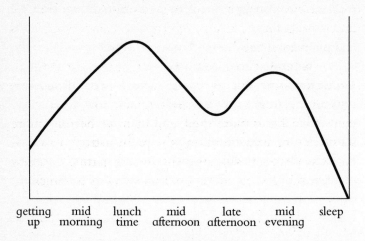

| getting up | mid morning | lunch time | mid afternoon | late afternoon | mid evening | sleep |

Where you find yourself subject to noticeable changes of mood on a regular basis, you may want to plot your own mood chart for a week, say, and then work out whether there are any traceable influences on those moods. For instance a big slump after lunch might be down to those regular bucketfuls of spaghetti carbonara you favour as your midday refuel. You could find it helpful to use my four terms to describe your mood at various points: wired, weary, poised and pacified, or you may want to keep asking yourself during the day: How are my energy vs tiredness levels now? and How are my calmness vs tension levels at this time? To increase your motivation, you want to find those periods where you feel poised, and both calm and energetic. Analyse all the factors surrounding those periods: What had you just been doing? Where were you? What time of day was it? Were you alone or with others? When had you last exercised and rested?

Use your best mood time to motivate yourself. If you know, for instance, that you feel energetic and calm that mid-morning, then that's the time to set goals for your new fitness programme, change of career, or mastery of diesel engine maintenance.

We women also know that our bodies go through monthly mood journeys. Just after our periods, we are typically at our most energetic. Ovulation, mid-cycle, tends to make us more tired, and then we become more sensitive – or worse – during the premenstrual period. It makes sense to schedule an event, such as starting on a new exercise programme, during our most energetic times.

At the mercy of your moods

Moods act as demotivators not just on the basis of the way they make us feel, but because we regard ourselves as being at their mercy. We increase the power a mood has over us by thinking that we are helpless to do anything about it. We feel overwhelmed by our moods to the extent that they prevent us being able to get up and motivate ourselves. Now while I'm not suggesting that you ignore a notice-able mood change and carry on regardless – indeed, this could be dangerous for your health – but there is a more constructive way in which we can view moods, I think.

That way is to view them as sources of information or feedback. That is really the function of a mood: to tell us that some biochemical changes are occurring in our bodies as a result of dehydration, diet, exercise levels, hormones or news of an exciting event. Our moods tell us what's working for us and what's not – what we are doing that's to our benefit and our detriment. And these reactions will very often be a mixture of the biochemical and the psychological, so we need to look at our moods from both perspectives.

When we take this more detached objective view of our moods, they become easier to manage.

Mood downers

Research shows – sorry, this is bad news for those of you with babies and young children, but you probably know this anyway – that the biggest cause of a low mood is sleep loss. But the effects of sleep deprivation may not always be that apparent. Janice, a working mother, talks about her experience:

> When my second child was four months old I went back to work. I remember going in to do an important presentation one day, having had one and a half hours' sleep. I'd drunk lots of espresso to try and make myself feel better. I entered the room and, horror of horrors, my face started to twitch slightly, but uncontrollably. I think it was the effect of exhaustion, wiring myself up with caffeine and trying to keep a brave face on it all, literally. I soldiered on through, and afterwards asked my colleagues if they'd noticed anything. I was convinced I must have looked psychopathic. 'No,' one of them said. 'You looked a bit strained that's all, but nobody noticed.' I decided to ask my boss if I could rearrange my work schedule temporarily so that I started early and finished early – I knew that if I could grab a couple of hours' rest late afternoon I could survive. I would spend lavishly on childcare till things settled down. That's the only way I could have got through that period without cracking up, I felt.

The trouble is that when we self-monitor, we often forget that human beings are essentially hedonistic; we do things that make us feel good and try to ignore things that make us feel bad. So we may completely ignore signals from our bodies that tell us we are experiencing tension and tiredness, and simply vent these reactions through our thoughts. For example, when I'm whacked because of working too hard, I'm usually rarely aware of physical reactions, instead I think poisonous thoughts along the lines of 'Poor old me, struggling on without an ounce of support . . .'

When people report low energy levels, they often also report low self-esteem, feelings of depression and a preoccupation with personal problems. Again, this is fairly consistently influenced by the time of day: in the morning personal problems will seem less pressing than later on in the afternoon. Remember that when you want to schedule a productive visit to your shrink: hit 4pm rather than 9.30am, on your way into work.

When we're trying to work out the cause of our moods, it's worth thinking about the influences of energy and tension. Energy levels are more likely to be affected by our biology: time of day, sleep, health and diet. Tension levels are more likely to be affected by our thoughts: what we perceive to be stressful, what we regard as being frustrating when we try to get what we want. But low energy levels make us vulnerable to the effects of tension: if you have a row with your partner at 11 o'clock in the morning or the same row at 11 o'clock in the evening, the later row is usually a lot more disturbing that the earlier one.

But *some* tension can increase motivation and energy. Particularly if you are the sort of control-fixated type person who leaves a lot of things to the last minute in order to feel especially in control. This type of person produces the goods under pressure. And yes, I'm afraid I would include myself in this category. You remember you have a deadline for your project, you have three days left to do it in, you feel energised and purposeful, with the slight tension of the deadline pressure. If, on the other hand, you do not start to tackle this substantial project until the evening before, the amount of tension you experience will in all probability throttle any energy you have, and make you feel completely exhausted at the insurmountability of the task ahead.

Mood uppers

I always feel somewhat pious and hypocritical when I need to write about healthy living. You see, when it comes to chocolate, I am a serial killer. In fact, at the time of writing, I am currently engaged in a personal research project into the complete lexicon of chocolate cake recipes. Under the guise of being a good mother, most weekends I rustle up yet another chocolate cake recipe discovery: with marmalade, pistachios, sour cream, Coca-Cola. You name it, we've had it. But hey, I use organic when I can and one of those pretend scientific reports the newspapers publish said recently that chocolate was good for you. So there.

There is no escape from it, though; to help maximise positive moods we must:

Exercise. Yes, yes, we all know practically everything you read about self-improvement bangs on about the need for exercise. You should know why. More than any other action or mood-altering substance you can take, exercise consistently makes people feel better. Across different types of depression, the one treatment that produces improvement in many different types of patient is exercise. Those endorphins just kick in and make us feel good. We start to create addictive, natural 'highs' for ourselves. And, of course, exercise increases our energy reserves, which means that we have more of them to fight off the bad effects of too much tension. Ken Branagh, the British protégé actor and director, tends to have a depressive personality. How does he keep moods at bay? Exercise, exercise, exercise.

To make it easier, you might want to exercise as early in the morning as you can. You might want to schedule it into your diary for the first six weeks till it becomes a habit. You might want to splash out on an expensive, local (within ten minutes, preferably) gym membership, or a personal trainer. You might want to plan an exercise programme that includes massage and aromatherapy treats as well. Or you might want to do what I did, which was to join a gym where the trainers are so gorgeous that you go there regardless of the pain, if only to get a whiff of all that testosterone.

You may have to negotiate very specifically with your partner about exercising at weekends, especially if you have children. Something along the lines of 'You will be free to go and watch Arsenal at home this afternoon, if you allow me to go to my 10.00am aerobics class; otherwise, I shall be going off to the 3.00pm one' normally works. In my experience, and counter to what all the advice says, doing this in a reasonable tone of voice never works at all . . .

Finally – and this is from a third party – two years ago some very close friends of mine, who felt they were sinking grumpily into middle age, got themselves a dog. They are much fitter and jollier, if more prone to early nights, as a result.

Check if we are under- or over-energised. When your moods are making you feel slightly depressed, you are suffering from a lack of energy. Exercising fairly vigorously should help here: aerobics, brisk walking, squash or fast swimming. When your moods are making you feel slightly anxious and agitated, then your energy has become tension and your remedies will need to be calming ones: a leisurely swim, Pilates, yoga or a gentle stroll.

Ration the usual culprits. Quick fixes like sugary treats, cigarettes, coffee, alcohol and drugs pay off in the short term, but in the longer term — and that can be just a few hours later — there will be a price to pay . . .

Rest enough. You may be very lucky and able to sleep for seven or eight hours every night, with a couple of hours to yourself most days. That's the ideal. If you don't, you might want to try meditation or catnapping after lunch; or, if you can't do that, just relax by closing your eyes and consciously tensing and relaxing your body bit by bit. Put yourself into a state of rest, if not sleep.

Like many people, I often have very early starts or overnight — and not very restful — stays in hotels. My strategy for dealing with these is lots of water, controlled caffeine, and walks outside in the fresh air during break-times. When I suspect I'm going to be tired, I always go for the early start and finish when scheduling my arrangements, so that my clients don't have to endure that late afternoon slump with me.

But this is very much a question of knowing your individual response to tiredness: when my partner's exhausted, he can't function at all in the morning, but will be raring to go by early evening. One theory says that this relates to levels of introversion and extroversion: introverts get more tired as the day goes on, particularly if they are being bombarded with a lot of external stimulation; extroverts get more stimulated as the day goes on, *especially*

if they are receiving that external stimulation bombard-
ment.

These preferences may also affect how we prefer to
recharge. The majority of we introverts will enjoy a quiet
potter in the kitchen, DIY corner, or bookshop, alone in
our recharging. The majority of you extroverts will enjoy
a group outing to the shops, a football match or the pub,
collectively recharging.

Eat well. This means eating breakfast, rather than a double
espresso and three Silk Cuts, and the two other main meals
of the day as well. It means five portions of fruit and veg
a day, and ensuring that at least 80 percent of what you eat
is healthy. It means monitoring your responses to carbohydrates and protein: I notice that large amounts of
carbohydrates of even the brown and wholemeal variety
make me feel more tired than a portion of fish, chicken or
meat, for instance. Many people experience the opposite;
that complex carbohydrates should provide a sustained
release of energy throughout the afternoon. If you find
that you slip into torpor after a meal, you may find that a
food sensitivity is at the root, and it's worth getting that
addressed.

Eating well means viewing good food as a friend not
an enemy, and enjoying the purchase and preparation of
meals as part of a good quality of life. It means taking
time to savour and digest your grub, and to enjoy its
sensual goodness. And, whoopee, eating well means that
the odd glass of Crozes Hermitage or Sauvignon carrying
health-giving antioxidants is not only acceptable, but positively encouraged! It also means eating organic as much as
possible.

Try alternatives. At the time of writing, the business
press has been reporting a scandal regarding trials of a

hair-restorer. Some 40 percent of those given the real thing improved by 40 percent, while those taking the placebo showed an improvement of 70 percent! Alternative treatments are sometimes worth sampling for their psychological boost, as much as anything else. Having said that, there is ample literature showing that alternative treatments are effective on a physical level, not just as a psychological response. For example, St John's wort can be as effective as antidepressants in many cases of depression (although don't mix the two), and it's now been well established that the herbs agnus castus and evening primrose oil are an effective means of controlling PMS-linked mood swings and some similar menopausal symptoms. The trick is to find the remedies and therapies that work best for you, and to locate a reputable practitioner who can help. If you have trouble believing that the vibes of crystals will make a difference to your life, then go for something with a body of research behind it, such as homeopathy or herbalism. Different things work for different people.

Mind over mood

When you view your moods as a source of information and feedback about things, you can use them to further your self-knowledge. For example, 'Oh, how very interesting, is this the mood I get in when I skip breakfast, drink three cups of espresso and have a row with Geoffrey in accounts?' A little self-knowledge goes a long way.

You can also lighten your mood and make it more motivating through the following:

Changing your environment. Go and work in another

place, feng shui your desk, take a few hours out to go down the beach or visit a street market. Just refresh very literally what you are seeing in your immediate world.

Alison is a writer, and she finds that the following 'shift' in environment works for her:

> I always find the books and articles I'm working on seem to move ahead dramatically after I've been on a long train journey. I may not be consciously working on or thinking about them, but I always return with a refreshed perspective. When I last got stuck on something I took half a day off and visited a nearby historical town, on the train, and returned with so many new ideas.

Reassociating yourself. Moods produce what's been called a 'state dependency', which affects how information is stored in our memory. It's the feeling that the poetic describe when they return to the place where they first fell in love, or less happily, that discomfort you get a year later when you accidentally bump into Geoffrey in accounts: while you've forgotten the actual row, seeing him reminds you of an unpleasant situation.

But we can make our associations compete with and outwit one another. So, if you are feeling in a sombre, under-energised mood, consciously give yourself ten minutes to mentally revisit a time where you felt completely irresistible, where you were strong and articulate and everyone present hung on your every word. And if that's never happened, then just create a mental scenario of how you would look, sound and feel if it did.

Ruminating less. I once worked with someone who, fortunately for his own sake, was self-employed. I say this because he was incredibly preoccupied with his own moods – to the extent that for a couple of days a month he would be unable to work, because he would regard his moods on those days as being so unhelpful. Having a puritanical work ethic, I used to be appalled. Was he psychologically sick? deeply sensitive? brilliant and understandably volatile? I somehow didn't think so.

No, his affliction was a tendency to be over-ruminative. He would dwell in great detail on how he was feeling and allow his mood to overwhelm him. He was over-precious in his treatment of himself as a result. You know that sort of person – only ever drinks herbal tea, and hot water and lemon. The world to him was a dangerous place in which a little flower like himself was constantly under threat. He was unattractively self-reverential.

He needed to do something, rather than wallowing in his vulnerable state. He needed to commit to some course of action, whether it was a distraction from his work or something tangential, like sitting down and doing his bookkeeping for the quarter. When I suggested this, he was shocked, yet he realised that every time he got into mood-rumination mode, the greater his memory of its power. He could control these moods by watching a funny film, listening to his favourite music, going out shopping or seeing friends.

The motivated mood

Once we're in a state where we feel ready to motivate ourselves, what can we do to make sure that we succeed in our plans?

Well, of all the various theories of motivation, the one that constantly seems to get results is *goal-setting*. Creating for ourselves a clear idea of what it is that we want to achieve and how we will know when we've got there. So it involves asking ourselves questions like 'What is it I want to do?', 'How long will it take?', 'What specifically will I achieve/produce at the end?', 'How will I know that I've achieved it?' and 'How will I feel/ look/sound/experience things differently?'

Goals work best when they are moderately difficult. Make them very hard and you may be setting yourself up for disappointment; make them too easy and you may well lose interest. It is the striving for what lies between what we currently have and what we want that keeps us well motivated.

Common sense will tell us, too, that when we are going for a big goal – running a successful business, losing five stone, completing a marathon, making an effective career change, for instance – then we need mini-goals en route. Again, it can be helpful to plot when we expect to achieve these and to make them as tangible, detailed, specific and as imaginatively vivid (through 'how will I feel/experience this' sort of fantasises) as we can.

Indeed, it is this imaginary, fantastical vision of goal-setting that is its most motivational aspect. Just targets alone do not motivate us – be honest, it's not just the five stone you want to lose, it's the great sex (potentially), amazing appearance (potentially), fabulous wardrobe (potentially), and irrepressible energy (potentially) that you will gain that are the real motivators. And, sometimes, if you're not quite clear about why you want something, such as money, career success or a new skill, then it's worth clarifying what it represents to you. There will be some imaginary element to it: one uppersonship, perhaps, or perceived freedom in the case of money; a sense of real, conventionally accepted achievement, perhaps, in the case of career success; or just a feeling of having mastered a true challenge in learning a new skill.

Writing down your goals and imagining how your life will be when you have achieved them are also helpful activities to maximise the likelihood of success.

Reality checking

Aren't there some klutzes working in self-improvement? I just love it when you read a magazine or newspaper article where the 'life-coach' or 'guru' gives advice like 'Get yourself goals in your professional life, personal life, fitness life, social life, spiritual life, and sexual life.' Haven't these people realised that life is about smelling the coffee, watching the sun rise, with the odd bit of success thrown in? Don't they realise that being unproductive can be gloriously fulfilling?

When we set ourselves too many goals in life, we start to suffer from the illusion that we are more in control of things than we really are. Realistically, it's wiser to prioritise two or three goals, which suit *your* life and *your* ideas about what's important. Leave some areas of your life to tick along without much effort, with just a gentle sense of direction. With too wide a range of goals, we can just end up feeling dissatisfied and inadequate. Edward works as an academic researcher at a university:

> We just moved a couple of streets away from a modern town house to a rambling period place. I had no idea of the impact it would have on what I thought I wanted. I started turning into my Dad, doing DIY all over the place and getting incredibly interested in gardening. My job didn't seem nearly so interesting by comparison, and the promotion I thought I wanted lost all its allure because it involved a

> *lot of foreign travel. I thought that after a year or two this might wear off, but it hasn't. I want to be a domestic god, and so I've actually moved roles so that I spend more time at home. It's just so pleasant; we have friends around a great deal and I've realised that conviviality is really a top priority for me.*

Feed me feedback, puhlease . . .

We can only gauge whether our judgements about reality are correct by asking other people about their judgements. Yes, that's pretty profound isn't it, for chapter two? What this means practically is talking to other people about the appropriateness of our goals, whether they are realistically achievable, and asking them for help and advice about our progress en route. I have a scary friend who always demands to know dreams and ambitions when we meet and schedules lunches a few months ahead for a progress report. She is controlling and obsessed with planning,but her generous spirit in doing this is greater than any of her faults.

When we ask people for feedback we need to make it easy for them. The magic question 'Is there anything I could be doing differently, here, do you think?' usually gets good results. Bear in mind, too, that the successful are often very flattered to be asked for advice: it's an acknowledgement of their wisdom.

Monitoring yourself

There's a kind, constructive way of being self-critical. It just involves asking what is working here, and what could be done differently? It is really important to ask these questions in this order, as when we identify what is working well, we can do more of it.

Now, laying it on the line, you're probably not going to achieve all your goals in life. So be it. But if you're confident about controlling your low moods and constructively using the good ones, your journey's going to be fun. Mood magic can make you motivated.

3 *When People Won't Play*

'Remember, a statue has never been set up in honour of a critic.'
Sibelius

There you are, all exhilarated by the marvellous new scheme that's motivating you, and you bump into an old friend you've not seen for some time. You enthusiastically describe your plans and she listens with a slight sneer on her lips that becomes stronger by the moment. 'Well,' she says, 'that all sounds fine and dandy, but how are you going to make money in the real world?' You feel deflated and a bit silly: you really wish you had kept your aims and hopes to yourself.

And that's the power of difficult people: they change our moods and make us feel that having entrusted them with our plans, we've now been made to look and feel ridiculous. Yet, it is most important that *we keep on entrusting*. For this is our only means of getting feedback about our ideas, before we put our plans into action. And sometimes it can be very sensible to seek out those we know to be cynical in order to get their responses – as a counterbalance to wildly optimistic tendencies that we may hold ourselves.

In this chapter I am going to look at ways of handling people who are acting as demotivators, both in terms of trying to get them to stop their unhelpful behaviour, and also – and I make no apologies about the rather pugilistic tone here – to see them for what they are: negative influences in our lives. At the end of this chapter,

I want you to feel that no matter how awkward the individual, you can rise above their negativity and fight on to follow your dreams.

After some general ideas about how to handle difficult people, we will look at four different and common types of detractor:

- negaholics
- criticisers
- withholders
- underminers

And if your heart is sinking at the prospect of all this investigation into the 'shadow side' of human beings, let me tell you that I aim to make this as jolly and robust a study as possible.

Difficult people, generally

If you are a fan of popular psychology, you'll know the main rule that relates to behaviour: start with yourself. It's always easier to question and change our own responses than those of other people, because we know ourselves best. When we are finding someone's behaviour deflating, it's worth asking several important questions of ourselves.

Is this a reflection of my own thoughts?

On presentation skills courses, honest participants often make comments like, 'I imagine everyone is going to think I don't know my stuff', or 'I suspect they're all thinking "How can someone her age talk to us about this"', or '"He's really boring", is what they're all thinking.' When we're honest, we will admit that most of us have a set of criteria that we constantly use to criticise ourselves. I'm particularly fond of criticising myself on the basis of lack of clarity, being rotund and smug, and being a bit too keen to entertain people. And when I'm finding a workshop tough-going, those are usually the criteria that I think the participants are going to use to criticise me.

Am I being paranoid?

Now sometimes, of course, I'll have a participant who instinctively – or through something I've said – realises that clarity is a top priority for me. And to undermine me – or perhaps it is something they do habitually as an undermining behaviour – they will sit there with a rather contrived 'puzzled' looking expression on their face. If I let this response go unquestioned, as the workshop goes on, I will perceive the puzzled expression to be getting stronger and stronger. So it works best for me to check my paranoia and ask the person whether they are a bit puzzled or whether this is just my perception. When they are using the response manipulatively, they always look surprised and play the innocent, saying that they were completely unaware that this was how they looked. By the way, I'm entrusting you with this disclosure. I'm certainly not inviting any of you to turn up at my workshops wearing puzzled expressions.

When you find someone difficult initially, and you're not sure whether it's your hyper-sensitivity or whether they really are difficult, then *asking other people about the meaning of their responses* can be a good reality vs paranoia check.

Am I being too self-critical?

So how do we clarify whether we are projecting our own criteria for self-criticism onto others? Common-sensically, *we need to be sure that we know what is most important to us in terms of how others view us.* Often, an honest answer to the question 'What would I least like to be found out not to be?' can provide this. Some frequent top concerns are 'I won't seem competent', 'I won't seem in control' 'I won't be attractive or likeable or acceptable' and 'I won't seem interesting and individual'.

When we find what amounts to a 'grand hang-up' – and no, we can't have them all – we can minimise their influence by acknowledging that they make us feel vulnerable and by verbalising this acknowledgement to others. Canny operators will say things like: 'I'm someone who's keen on knowing lots about my subject, so if I miss anything important out, please forgive me' or 'I like things to run as smoothly as possible, so if anything goes wrong, don't worry about me getting flustered'. You are taking out an insurance policy here, against those people who can instinctively sense where you are vulnerable and will use that against you. By the way, in my experience, these types tend to be isolated individuals with few real good relationships. If you think they are everywhere, then that paranoia needs attention of the psychiatric kind . . .

To check a tendency to be too self-critical it's also a good idea to *confess to someone about your Achilles heel.* Tell a friend that you know you're unrealistically perfectionist, or really hung up on controlling everything, and ask them to let you know when they think these tendencies are being detrimental to what you're trying to achieve. Who knows, they may welcome the opportunity to confess back.

Do I want peace at any price?

Like me, you may think it's pleasant to live and work in an atmosphere created by people who value consensus and reasonable behaviour. Or you may think this is a wimpily compromising goal, bearing in mind that human beings are, above all else, self-seeking and aggressive. In which case, you may need to prove your case be one of those people who terrorises the rest of us with their punchy approach.

Now a certain amount of conflict is inevitable when a group of human beings get together to do anything, be it live as a family, work as a team or study as a group. And some of us have a dread of conflict that makes us pushovers to others, either because we acquiesce to their demands immediately, or go out of our way to avoid any kind of conflict and therefore become manipulated by the conflict seekers.

Take, for example, Sam, who works in banking:

> *I grew up in a household where there was a lot of conflict between my parents and I'm not at all comfortable with it. I was always trying, unsuccessfully inevitably, to make peace between them. When I started work I realised that meetings were, in many people's eyes, battlegrounds for dominance. If I didn't get over this fear of conflict I was not going to be able to contribute very much. So I made myself speak up and express my views – on just one topic per meeting to begin with – then, as my confidence built, I spilt forth on whatever I felt strongly about. I'd say I'm still really most comfortable with establishing consensus on things and I do that quite skilfully I think. Indeed, someone told me the other day I was regarded as the most successful non-chairing chairman in the whole company.*

Am I taking things too personally?

Where the prospect of conflict worries us, we have *to deper-sonalise what is going on.* We have to think about conflict in terms of discussion over issues, rather than anything that has a personal agenda behind it. The debate is over situations, and the different ways that people interpret a situation. Remember: you are defining it one way, while they are defining it another. If they seem to be attacking you, ignore it and find out more about how they are defining the situation – what they see as top priorities, threats to what they want to achieve, and possibilities to help the situation.

Aggressive people are scared of something, otherwise they would not need to be aggressive. Asking people what they are concerned about may identify this, or ask them to describe further any imminent threats they may perceive to the situation. Where you have it in your powers to allay their fears, you have an end to the conflict.

The best way to overcome a fear of conflict is to *start expressing your own opinions about things.* This needn't mean at the expense of everyone else's opinions. A tentative 'I suspect there might be others here who think differently' can show that you are aware that your opinion might be a lone one. Give yourself time limits – the first half hour of a meeting, say – during which you give yourself the task of expressing a definite viewpoint. Even if that opinion is on the superiority of the filter coffee over the instant, that is still a viewpoint. Where you haven't got much of an opportunity to express opinions at work, you may want to join some sort of adult study group, where opinions are expressed and encouraged as part of the learning process. There is always the local debating society, a political party or some sort of campaigning group, such as Greenpeace, for instance. Shock your friends, too, by saying what you really think about the latest trendy bar or restaurant in your neighbourhood.

People who are really good company are often comfortable expressing extreme views for provocation and entertainment value, without any sort of underlying personal agenda to others present.

Less obviously, I suspect that if a pacifist and conflict avoider takes up a martial art, then it may have all sorts of unexpected benefits for their confidence to handle conflict in all sorts of situations. *Ah, so.*

Defeating the difficult

Above all else, *you must believe that you can handle difficult* people. If you can't do that, believe that you can have a real stab at it. View the way you handle them as an experiment where you get to develop your skills as an amateur Freud, researching and helping them at the same time. Actually, there's no excuse for anyone believing they can't handle difficult people these days. Not when authors like me are churning out books like this in their thousands every day.

It is very helpful to be able to *keep cool*. Losing your rag is bad for your health, the brain gets aroused, causes the heart to beat faster and, repeatedly doing this keeps the body in a more constantly aroused state. Body language, facial expression and voice are best kept cool, calm, measured and controlled.

I learned this myself many years ago. I was a volunteer in an organisation that helped people in crisis in Central London. One of our clients went berserk in a small office, armed with his Alsatian and a large knife. Despite being only about twenty-four, I was in charge and so it was my job to go in there and help the client. This was a very steep learning curve, despite all the guidelines I'd been given about what to do in such a situation. I walked in very slowly, shut the door and asked him repeatedly to put the knife away and to calm the dog. I stayed for about five minutes, gave him a few minutes to cool down by himself and then went back in. As I recall, I exited and left him in there three times, before the knife was eventually put away. After that, it was remarkable how quickly he calmed down, became reasonable and left the premises.

When we give ourselves the quick mental instruction to relax and reassure other people through our behaviour, we often end up doing these things to ourselves, too.

Talking it out

Some of us are so habitually defensive that it may pay to practise describing what is happening in a situation, rather than defending our role in that situation. Get a friend to fire some nasty questions at you and practise forming answers that calmly describe the situation rather than going on the defensive. You are just going for a fairly neutral, friendlyish account of the facts as you see them. I frequently train lawyers in this exercise and, as you can imagine, they find it very useful.

Assertiveness training techniques can also be helpful. The formula of *describing, disclosing and generating solutions* is quite easy to remember. This is along the lines of 'When you criticise me constantly in front of your mother, I feel upset and I wondered whether we should have her over less often, you could stop criticising me, or do you have any other suggestions?'

The 'broken record technique' of endlessly repeating a key message will eventually get through to people. Linked to this, some of us need to practise saying 'no', especially if we are peaceably inclined. Using a mollifier, of the 'You're probably not going to like this, but I have to say no' variety, often makes it easier.

Discussion of interpretations of the situation can be fruitful, as long as both parties are open about what they want. Where you reach a complete impasse, you may want to clarify and try to better understand one another's definitions, perhaps breaking to come back another time. If there is anything at all on which you can agree – some very small detail or piece of action, or some underlying principle that you both hold dear – then you will succeed in lessening the conflict. Sometimes, though, there is no alternative to the 'you are seeing it this way, and I am seeing it that way' scenario, and you may have to agree to differ for the time being. It's a cliché, I know, but time, that old healer, may need to play its part then.

People in my line of work often like to use aphorisms, and one of the most popular is that 'There are no difficult people, just difficult behaviour'. Sorry, but no. There are some individuals with destructive behaviour habits, which they repeated use to blight the lives of the rest of us. No mincing of words, or Pollyanna generosity here: these are difficult people.

Negaholics

Oh, we've all encountered them, haven't we? Those grim-faced carriers of buckets of cold water, who regard themselves as devout realists – the select few who understand the bleak nature of true prediction. They want to put you on a downer. Take Howard's position. He works in IT:

> I work in a company where the mission statement is 'We innovate for our customers' and we are meant to be working in a culture where inventive thinking takes priority over failure. But my boss doesn't seem to get this. Every suggestion I make he pooh-poohs, pointing out all the pitfalls that lie ahead and what will certainly go wrong. I've tried going above his head to his boss, but I really need my boss's backing for me to turn my ideas into projects. It's not just me who gets this negative treatment – everyone else does too. We are all terribly demoralised and we know our department has now got a reputation for efficiency, but is otherwise regarded as a very dull place. Our boss came here from an operations role where his job required him to be incredibly sensitive to every pitfall; it seems he can't make a transition to seeing that a different perspective is required in this role.

So, what to do about negaholics? Listening can work, as can noting down their comments in a notebook, a somewhat intimidating device, particularly if they are held responsible for your appraisal. You've then got those scathing comments to show human resources. Well, it's sometimes a war out there, isn't it?

Paraphrasing negaholic comments, especially when

there are other people present, can be a good way of high-lighting the intention behind the comments. For example, 'So you don't think it will work because the costs involved would be too high', 'You think the deadline is unrealistic because it would create a lot of pressure for us to produce results by June' and 'You judge the estimate of how many people required on the team to be too few by about three, and we just don't have three extra people available'. I'm sure I don't have to spell out the fact that the more detailed your paraphrasing, the fuller the damnation sounds . . .

When you know someone to be predictably negaholic in meetings, you might want to go and see them before-hand, asking them for their view. This can often be very helpful if your shades are of the rose-tinted variety. You can adjust your case to incorporate some of their objections, and to provide alternatives. But some negaholics don't do it on a one-to-one basis – their goal is public humiliation. In this case, you may want to incorporate into your presenta-tion the fact that you are expecting them to point out the pitfalls and look forward to hearing them – their realistic perspective always being welcome, of course. Now I realise that this may sound somewhat toadying, but your aim here is to take them out of the equation using psychological weaponry.

For obvious reasons, it's *sooo* easy to go on the defensive when preparing a case for a negaholic in the audience. And then the problem is that those positaholics in the audience all wonder 'Why did they make that case so defensively?' But, it's very helpful to consider all of the objections that might be raised, to back up all your ideas and proposals with good reasoning, case histories and examples, and, above all, to be absolutely clear in your argument about the *positive* benefits that will result from your ideas. Then all the downer objections can be considered, counter-reasoned and politely dismissed with an 'And, can I repeat, this will bring us huge benefits in terms of . . .' Hope persuades people as effectively as fear. And it's a far more attractive emotion to which to appeal.

Finally, on the subject of the unfortunate negaholics, remember that these are not happy people. I once had a negaholic work for me for a short time, and not only was she negative, but she was angry and resentful. She worked for me at a time when a lot of changes in my life made me rather vulnerable. The only way I could cope with her downer tendencies was to be hugely and relentlessly cheerful in her presence and to avoid her as much as possible the rest of the time. When she saw that I was undaunted by her relentless pessimism, she used less of it, privately thinking to herself, I suspect, that her employer was completely off her trolley.

Criticisers

Think negaholics are bad? What about the criticisers. Here's Sally's experience with her husband Bill, when she was setting up her own business.

Anything I do really gets criticised. Sometimes I feel that I've lost my sense of humour, because it's often in the form of sarcasm or jokiness. So, for instance, if I'm planning what I'm going to try and do when the children are both in school, he'll say things like 'Oh, so you're going to be Nicola Horlick, then are you?', and when I rush to defend my plans he'll back down with an 'only joking'. It is criticism, but in a kind of veiled form and actually all the more hurtful because of it.

The worse type of criticisers are usually relentless perfectionists, who put themselves constantly under pressure because they can never be good enough, and who apply these same Everest high standards to others. When they're grumpy with themselves for inadequate performance, they may well take it out on others, attacking them instead of facing up to their own problems. Being a punch bag for a relentless perfectionist is no joke.

The best attitude to take with such people is that 'all feedback is fascinating'. And I mean fascinating in the way that David Bellamy sees an interesting piece of wildlife or Patrick Moore surveys an astronomical constellation. This is not personal, it is just interesting feedback. Often comments like 'how interesting' or 'that's a fascinating response' can show that you are taking this scientific position.

You may want to check that you have their meaning exactly. So paraphrase what they have said in the way that you've understood it: 'Ah, so you're under the impression that I'm going to try and be a fund manager in the City, are you?' and check that this is what they meant. I'm sure you've realised that this is a pretty mean way of flushing out hidden agendas. However, the more open you are about your feelings to these hidden agendas – 'Mmmm, I feel quite concerned that I've got you confused here' – the more you highlight the criticiser's duplicitous nature.

You might want to ask them about their motivation; again, approach it quite factually, with a 'That's an interesting response. Why would you say that?' And you might want to agree with some of the criticism, or at least allow them some validity: 'Yes, I can see how you might come to say that – it could be partly true'. In all these instances you are not giving the negative criticiser what they want: a hurt or wounded reaction. Instead you are entering into a clarification of meaning and understanding with them. Sneaky, eh?

You can also turn the situation around, by becoming slightly counsellorish. In other words, 'Mmmm, you obviously feel quite strongly about what I'm doing here' shows empathy and concern for the criticiser, if they are manipulative, this won't be what they are expecting at all. But, most effectively, you can use the killer technique of asking them for constructive suggestions, along the lines of 'What do you think I could do differently?', 'How could I put it right?' or 'What alternative plans would you positively suggest?' If the criticiser is unable to put a positive tack in any way, shape or form, then they've been rumbled. Avoid them as much as possible, or move out.

Just a quick reminder, which is helpful in any sort of criticism-giving, be it to ourselves or others. It always works best when the positives are identified and acknowledged first and then the shortcomings are considered.

Withholders

When Helen was beginning the second year of her studies, she encountered the follow example of withholding:

> I'm studying for a PhD and I'm having a lot of problems with my supervisor. She just doesn't react much to anything I do or say. I don't know whether it is because she wants me to make all my own decisions – I think I do that anyway. But she's just very distant and inscrutable. I don't know whether our relationship will develop sufficiently for me to feel helped and encouraged by her through this long period of study or whether I should ask to change to someone else . . .

Yes, this is the super-cool cookie. The person who knows inscrutability can be mysterious and compelling, but also that those of us expressive, desperate-to-please-and-amuse types will be fazed by a lack of reaction and try even harder to get a favourable response. Yes, if you think this sounds written from the heart, you'd be right. I've banged my head against that particular stone barrier several times.

Talking to others should be easy, shouldn't it? Except that we all expect different things from communication. I frequently find myself in the position of being misunderstood by others, who believe that I am totally in agreement with them because what I've intended to say through my nodding head and smiling expression and mmms of encouragement, is 'Yes, I'm listening, please go on talking'. But my conversational partners tend to have taken these indicators to be a comment on *content,* meaning that I am wholeheartedly in agreement with everything being said. It can be embarrassing having to explain what your behaviour signals meant, as opposed to leaving it that you are in complete agreement with his or her views on capital punishment.

So if you suspect that you are being manipulated and demotivated by someone withholding a response from you, it's best to be as upfront as possible. A confession like 'I would really like to get some clearer understanding about your views/ feelings on this' or 'I need more approval than many people, can you tell me what you think of this so far' will be disarming and should provoke some reaction. You may even want to go as far as to say: 'I find you very hard to read, and I need clear feedback, so can you please give me some?'.

Another device that can be helpful is to get these cool customers actually physically involved in whatever it is that you are doing together. And no, I don't mean that you try and coerce them into giving you a hug or a stroke, or whatever it is that you feel you need. What I mean is this: if you are planning to do something, or have been getting some ideas together, for a paper, for instance, you actually show them, give them the paper and ask them if they would mind coming back with their comments. That way you are not pressurising them, but you are giving them something tangible to which they can react.

Sometimes, people who appear to be withholding do not actually intend to do so. They may just come from low-reacting families, or simply believe that in being very contained and calm, the effect they create is to calm and soothe others, rather than worrying the hell out of we performing types because we see and hear no applause . . .

Underminers

Lyn, a marketing manager in a law firm, has met with a different type of resistance from yet another group of negative thinkers – the underminers:

> There's a woman in my office who I think is talking about me a great deal behind my back. I keep getting odd reports from other people that they've heard projects I'm working on are not going well, or that I was unhappy about things that I've not given an iota of thought to. I think she knows that in my role, reputation is terribly important and she seems to be using this as a means of demoralising

me. It's very difficult to deal with, because, of course, it's all
hearsay.

It's easy to see how the old paranoia can kick in here, because underminers are often subtle and covert in their tactics: doing things like sending people on remedial training courses, supervising work much too closely, or inventing stories about your crimes and misdemeanours that you rarely get to hear about, directly.

The main thing to remember here is that the underminer's goal is your reaction. They sense an Achilles heel and they are going to pursue you until they find it, and can strike it, often because you are threatening to them or they are jealous of you. So you have to learn to act in ways that are opposite to what you feel.

When the underminer announces that you are being sent on the basic computer skills course, even though you are thoroughly computer-literate, rather than look shocked, act thrilled to be given this opportunity to learn and have a jolly day out of the office.

When they supervise your work much too closely, implying that you are a half-wit who can't be left alone to do anything (with the intention of claiming all the glory for the project), don't go into a huff. Instead, thank them profusely for taking such an interest in your development and progress, and lavish praise about how good it is to work so closely with them. Innocently e-mail all personnel two levels above your boss to inform them of your progress on this project, and you might even mention what a gem your boss has proved to be by giving you so much of his/her undivided attention and time in a busy department.

And when reports and lurid tales of your sexual exploits

following the team-meeting-that-ended-up-in-the-night-club reach you, thank the underminer profusely and in front of everyone else for improving your image. You were aware that people thought you were some sort of Bridget Jones-type frump, and now everyone knows that you are one hot biscuit.

You get the gist: whatever they do to undermine you, whatever detrimental activity they can drum up, spin it so that it sounds like you were really pleased about what they've done. Almost anything anybody does – short of convictable offences – can be interpreted as beneficial for them in the long-term. If you ensure that they don't get the desired response, the undermining will stop pretty quickly.

There you go – all types of difficult people sewn up for easy dealing. Simply remember that most difficult people are behaving that way because they are jealous of your vision, enthusiasm, commitment, energy, positive purpose, friends and/or creativity. No one can take that away from you.

4 *Growing Creativity*

'Imagination is more important than knowledge.'
Einstein

Creativity's got a rather magical, mystical quality about it, hasn't it? We speak in reverential tones about a famous artist being 'creative', but we may use the same word in a more frustrated tone of voice when we describe someone whose behaviour is beyond our understanding. Oh yes, the word 'creative' covers a whole multitude of meanings.

And why is creativity important to motivation? Well, I often refer to the state known as 'flow' in my writing. Just to remind you, this is a state where we perform optimally: where our attention is utterly focused on what we are doing, we lose track of time, we are relaxed yet energetic and purposeful, and we feel a huge sense of satisfaction when we finish our activity. Athletes and their coaches often refer to this state as being 'in the zone'. All sorts of activities may create this state for us: pruning the roses, love-making, theorem-solving or shopping. And because of our sense of entire engagement and satisfaction in this state, it is the most motivating one in which we can be. The more flow we experience, the more we want to experience. It is the state we enter into when we are being creative. And in these terms, the word 'creative' does not have to involve anything even remotely artistic.

When we are being creative, we become extremely interested in what we are doing. We feel hopeful and optimistic. We are full of the possibility of achievement.

We have a sense of living life to its fullest degree. Our performance benefits greatly from all these psychological advantages. Logically, then, we might think that it would be worth our education system and workplace maximising opportunities for us to be creative, with the benefits that would ensue. Realistically, though, most of us know that this is not the case. We shall examine why later.

In this chapter then I look at what creativity means, the myths people hold about it, and how all of us can increase creativity in our lives to motivate us further.

That creative word

Two people look at the same piece of modern art at the Pompidou Centre in Paris. One says, 'Marvellous, how moving', while the other one says, 'What a mess, my three-year-old could make more sense than that'. Now there seems to me that there are two aspects of the word creativity that confuses us: the first aspect is originality, and the second is the value of the creation.

When we are creative we make something. We bring into being something that didn't exist before. These days, it is extremely difficult to make something that is utterly original: usually someone will have created a part of the plot before or designed an aspect of the mathematical formula, previously. So the originality often comes in seeing something differently from other people, or putting things together in a way that people haven't experienced before. Post-it notes, Tom Jones' revival as a trendy icon, Tracey Emin's unmade bed are all examples of this type of original creativity. When the visitor at the Pompidou Centre says 'Marvellous, how moving' – and means it – we can surmise that something about the way the artist sees the world mirrors the way the visitor sees it.

Whatever we create needs to have some value. This may be purely value for ourselves; there are creative writers, for instance, who use what they produce solely to help themselves make sense of their world and experience. And then there are the likes of Danielle Steel and Stephen King, whose creations are valued and bought by millions of people around the world. In the art and literary worlds, fortunately, the word 'value' does not always mean 'commercially successful'. So innovative artists and writers are sponsored for their 'originality' value rather than their market value. The visitor at the Pompidou Centre who sees the piece of art as a mess is not seeing any value, *for themselves*, in what they are looking at.

The question of what criteria determines the value of creative offerings is a huge one. And it's a question that has spawned the industries of art and literary criticism, fashion writing and advertising awards. People demonstrate many of the tendencies that I described in my last book, *Irresistibility,* when they choose their criteria: herd tendency with ideas like: 'If that art collector bought it, then the artist must be good'; or, scarcity value: 'There are only two of those designs available so they must be precious.'

When Freud said that there were two really important contributors to happiness, love and work, I think what he was really talking about creativity. Creating something that you have absolutely loved making: a garden, a baby, a cake, a business or a painting, for example, seems to me to be at the very essence of what it is to be human. Yet in psychology, the study of creativity is given scant attention, and that's probably because of some of the myths surrounding the subject.

Myths of creativity

The abounding myths about creativity make it a rather marginalised subject: we don't talk about it much, there doesn't seem to have been much written about it, and not many companies run training courses in it . . . Let's have a look at some of these myths; they may be limiting your own use of your creativity.

Creativity isn't 'scientific'

This is a very popular myth and one that has perhaps limited the psychological explorations into creativity. Psychology often tries hard to get itself taken seriously as a science. For what it's worth, my view of this phenomenon is that it should give it up and resign itself to being an art.

Describing creativity as 'non-scientific' involves black and white, 'either/or' thinking. People are *either* analytical *or* creative, they are *either* artistic *or* scientific, they are *either* objective and rational *or* subjective and emotional. Ah, if only life were that simple, categorical and easy to sort out; a quick consideration of how we think will disabuse us of this fantasy.

Our brains like patterns of ideas to make sense of things. We use these patterns to analyse. So analysis is based on things that have happened previously and what happens when we analyse is that we survey a current situation, and see how it meshes with our current pattern of ideas. If what we survey doesn't fit into our current pattern of ideas, we may reject it, allow it gradually to influence our pattern of ideas, or let it simmer away in the unconscious.

So while analysis has the great advantage of organising and structuring for us, it is limiting, in that it uses existing patterns of ideas that are in our brains, and it surveys *what currently exists*.

When our brains work creatively, we lose rigid patterning and often become much more asymmetrical in our thinking. While we may start by surveying what it is, we move to speculate about what could be: leaps of connections between ideas occur. We use more unconscious patterning; ideas come from our unconscious mind to make sense of information and experience. Now when we're talking about the unconscious mind, we're in an area that is largely speculative, but I bet that some of you have had similar experiences to my friend Rose, a writer:

> I've often found that after a particularly unproductive day, where I've just produced maybe a thousand words and I'm feeling dissatisfied with myself, that while I sleep my mind seems to solve the problems. I'll wake up feeling refreshed, with a head full of cogent ideas and a good sense of clear direction about the book. It's marvellous, really, that the mind has the power to do this guiding.

We are all capable of analytical and creative thinking, though our skills can become rusty. Geniuses, like Einstein, often describe playing imagination games, honing their creativity to think about the power of possibility. Great art involves analysis and study of technique: great science involves generation and design of hypothesis or 'what might be'. A creative approach can be brought to anything: you just have to consider how mathematicians and computer scientists created the internet to realise the truth of this statement.

Creativity lacks structure

'Is it creative or is it a mess?' I think, as I survey my four-year-old's latest painting. Being a soft touch, I usually choose the former judgement. People often view structure and the chaos of creativity as being incompatible. But many forms of structure can help to encourage creativity and fulfil a creative instinct: the great plot of a novel, the understanding of composition in the painting, the order and method in the kitchen that produces culinary glories. Structure creates meaning for us: and for our creativity to have meaning for anyone else, other than ourselves, it will need shape and form.

It's important to remember that it's our use of analysis that causes us to believe that structure is incompatible with creativity.

If our patterns of ideas are very rigid, if we are stuck with ideas that things *must* be done in a certain way, routines and rules adhered to, then we will certainly limit our creative potential. We will not be able to allow new information and experiences to influence our sense-making so that we can think innovatively.

Creativity is dangerous

Being the sort of person with a relentless desire for continual self-improvement, I have an arts and a science degree. When I started my MSc, I found life in my study group very difficult indeed. I would throw myself into discussion to be greeted with quizzical expressions and little response. One evening a lecturer was listening in on our discussion and at coffee time she took me aside. 'Are you having difficulties in the group?' she asked. 'Em, yes,' I replied gratefully. She went on, 'I think it's to do with your background and orientation. You are very divergent in your contribution, you leap all over the place, and a lot of your ideas are associative. Most of the people in your group are quite convergent in their thinking, they like ideas to be sequential, orderly and moving towards a resolution.'

This was a revelation to me, and explained why people had been looking at me like I was on a different planet. I thought the group discussion was about brainstorming; the rest of the group thought it was about problem-solving – hence the incompatibility.

In places where preserving the status quo is very important, creativity may be seen as dangerous. It involves challenging preconceived ideas, imagining alternative scenarios and creating new and flexible structures. For organisations, the irony is that while many of them desperately need to retain and promote creative people to cope with constant uncertainty and change, they are the very people who are most difficult to manage – because, of course, 'manage' means command and control.

Creative people are unhappy

Studies of creative geniuses, such as Anthony Storr's *The School of Genius,* often show that these individuals spent a lot of time in solitude in their childhood. Presumably this was where they were able to develop their imaginations. This doesn't, of course, necessarily mean that they were unhappy: just that circumstances gave them an opportunity to practise creativity.

In the US, Dr Martin Teicher has recently published a study that looked at the brain scans of hundreds of children who had suffered neglect, physical and sexual abuse. The researchers discovered that the corpus callosum, the nerves linking the two sides of the brain, were up to 40 percent smaller than average in the abused children. This results in impeded communication between the two sides of the brain, with the child spending more time residing in one side than the other. This creates a lack of balance between the right hemisphere, where creative and emotional thought occurs, and the left, where rationality and language processing occurs. It might be likely, then, that unhappiness causes these children to spend more time in the right hemisphere, where they miss the logic of the other side of the brain. Presumably these children are more likely to grow into creative, unhappy adults.

Herein, perhaps, lies the foundation of the myth. Creative people from unhappy backgrounds are obviously much more likely to become unhappy adults. So many creative geniuses are famously unhappy – think of van Gogh, for example, or Sylvia Plath. But is there necessarily a correlation? I think not. I have encountered – as I am sure you have – wonderfully fulfilled people who are managing to earn a good living and express themselves thoroughly through their creativity. Most of them seem to view themselves as exceptionally lucky to be paid for doing what they love. While I would not describe these individuals as unhappy, there is a restlessness about them and a drive to create. This motivation must come from a vision or idea of what could be in relation to how things actually are. They are motivated to create to close that gap. Without the gap, there would be no creativity. So smugness and complacency are not really compatible with creativity: and if these individuals have these feelings about their lives generally, when it comes to their work they have to set up a contradiction between what is and what could be, in order to create.

Creative people are egomaniacs

Creative people are not egomaniacs, but they are usually enormously enthusiastic about what they do and can sometimes talk about little else. They're not interested in dominating you with their egos, but are just bursting to tell you about their passion. Take my friend Tony, who is a creative genius. He is a science professor who invented a method of diagnosis for thyroid conditions that revolutionised treatment globally. He is also a consummate classical pianist. He is dad to five children and has set up hugely successful science projects for children during the school holidays. His wonderful partner Stephanie helps him in all this. Being in Tony's company is extraordinarily exhilarating – he doesn't stop talking about his latest involvement and opinions. But he's not for the fainthearted. But egomaniac? Not a bit of it.

Creative products that are valued by a lot of people – such as great novels, pieces of music or films – will touch a common chord. Now I don't want any of you, especially readers who are familiar with my work, to think I've completely lost the plot here. But I'm increasingly of the view there is something like a collective unconscious into which ideas go, are circulated and then picked up or ignored. It's a sort of earthspace rather than a cyber one: the ether picks up our thoughts and whirls them around until they find another suitable human destination. If you think this is bunkum, and you're possibly quite right, then you must concede that human beings have feelings and fantasies in common with each other, and that these could create a kind of 'collective unconscious'. Either way, great creations reach into our 'collective unconscious' and touch us.

Having a sense of what is really going on in others and what will touch them is not the attribute of an egomaniac. Rather, it is the talent of someone who has a great deal of attention and receptivity to give to other human beings and their collective concerns.

Creativity is all about Eureka moments

The drama of the Eureka moment is a powerful one: you know, you're just strolling along and *pow!* a brilliant plot hits you, or you just wake up one morning and *zowee!* you've completely recreated your business in one fell swoop . . . We do undoubtedly have these moments, where there are powerful leaps of connection between ideas that suddenly compute into something creative and exciting, but creative processing also has a much gentler pace, in which information and experience gradually shifts into our existing patterns of ideas and changes them.

Some of you are no doubt thinking, 'Well, I've never had a Eureka idea in my life, I wouldn't know one if it hit me on the nose, I can't be creative.' And this brings up another misconception about creativity – the belief that we are either born that way, or terminally uncreative with no hope of that ever changing. But all of us are creative; some of us just need to nurture it more. Nurturing creativity does not involve an educational system that gives children gold stars for sitting quietly in class and not asking questions. Unfortunately, that's the route our society chooses to take. Sure, we can have sympathy for the over-worked teachers, but rewarding children for passivity is hardly going to foster creativity.

Creativity has to be trained and developed. All of us are capable of creating marvellous things when we've practised a great deal, and given the time in which to do so, we can all express ourselves creatively. What's more, it doesn't matter how old we are. Creativity is so much at the core of who we are as human beings that even if it is very rusty, it can still express itself with some encouragement. Your creativity needs to be nurtured and to be given good conditions in which to thrive.

A lot of creativity is about synthesis: putting together two different ideas to form an original outcome. The Post-It note is a good example of this – the need for notes matched with stickiness. The more you know about the area in which you are working, and develop skills to work in it as efficiently as possible, the more likely you are to have a creative breakthrough. And that breakthrough is as valid if it is a slow simmer to boiling point, rather than the drama of a Eureka moment.

Increasing your creativity

If you want to live your life more creatively and thereby feel more motivated, here are some ideas:

Get uninhibited. Many people hold back from creative expression because they are afraid of being wrong and looking silly. Maybe they hold a self-image that tells them they are very intelligent or intellectual so they can't risk saying or doing anything that doesn't support this. Oh dear, this is sad way to live your life.

You could counteract these tendencies by deliberately learning something unusual and challenging where you know the odds are that you will get it wrong. Skiing would be an example for me. For my partner it would be wild-flower painting. When we learn anything new, it can change the way we view lots of other areas of our lives.

Where you are taking yourself too seriously and are

afraid of blowing this self-image, it helps to see yourself instead as an experimenter. You can still take yourself quite earnestly as an experimenter but, crucially, you are an experimenter who doesn't know what the answers will be, or the end result. So if you make wild suggestions or come out with wacky ideas that has everyone else sitting with shocked expressions on their faces, what the hell, it was only an experiment . . .

Now I don't want to go all Californian on you, but what we are talking about here folks, is, inescapably your inner child. That little bit of you that is still inquisitive, fun seeking, naughty, slightly rebellious, full of *joie de vivre* and enthusiasm. Yes, and I'm going to tell you that you have to nurture it, let it out. Take it to the fair, the bowling alley, Centre Parks, let it play. Maggie, a lawyer, confessed:

> The other day, we were walking in the park as a family and my partner commented on how marvellous it was the way our seven-year-old skipped. He asked me if I remembered doing that and said he wished he still could. I threw down a skipping challenge and within ten seconds, all of us were skipping through the park. Now we are both in our forties, and we were quite smartly dressed, so we did attract some odd looks. We roared with laughter, probably embarrassed our son no end, but I haven't felt so exhilarated for years. I heartily recommend skipping therapy.

Get good sex. No doubt there are some brilliantly creative celibates around, but sexuality and creativity are closely linked. Indeed, there's a powerful argument that making babies is our most creative act. Many mystical writers believe there to be a connection between spiritual, creative and sexual fulfilment. Certainly a sense of transcendence, where we almost 'lose ourselves' to some greater energy characterises all three states. By getting good sex, I don't mean just a quick bit of rumpy-pumpy – though of course that has its merits at times – I mean the intimacy, sensuality and sense of connection that one gets from sex with love. Good for keeping those inhibitions at bay and boosting self-esteem, too.

Spend more time by yourself. We are more likely to develop our creativity and also to generate new ideas when we spend time by ourselves. Brainstorming in groups is rarely a great way to increase creativity, as it just encourages people who like dominating to express their ideas. If you don't have anything that you do by yourself, take up creative writing, cooking, piano-playing, meditation, bath-soaking – anything that means you regularly have periods of time alone.

I suspect many of us are more exhausted than we need to be, just because we don't have enough recharge times where we are in solitude: absolutely alone in a place, reflecting quietly on what is happening in our lives and how we can shift those patterns of ideas to accommodate this. All of us are too busy doing things, or spending time in crowded public transport where we feel physically encroached upon but psychologically very lonely indeed. I'm not suggesting you become a hermit or anything as drastic as that, just that you take time, occasionally, to sit quietly and ruminate on what you are doing and why.

Face your doubts and fears. When we decide to be more creative, we are, in the truest sense of the words, putting ourselves forward. We are saying to the world, 'This is what I make, do you like it?' And those doubts and uncertainties that we manage to control when we fail to venture, will start to nag. Concerns like, 'Will the world reject me?', 'Am I good enough?' and 'Will people think I'm an upstart?' will undoubtedly try to head off any attempts to be creative. In fact, our inner critic may get itself turned up to high in order to blast us with negative comments.

So how to counteract these unhelpful voices? Well, from what I've observed with people who want to write, but can't, there is no point at all in denying that these voices are there. Get the little demons out and have a look at them, using my favourite method of all: draw them, like cartoons, on some paper. Give them speech bubbles, too, to write down their barbs. Stick them on one side of the page. On the other side of the page, create their alter ego, an angel or a god, who is your prime champion and gives you messages that are exactly the opposite to those of the demon. Draw a line between the two of them and have a good look at that dynamic. You are illustrating a contra-dictory, oppositional pull in your mind, and you may never resolve it. But having made it concrete, you can at least decide where you are at any given point on the continuum between the two opposing voices. And having created a champion to talk to the negative voice, you can argue back when it gets too strong.

Here's an example:

Develop your creative thinking. Even though you may not want to write, a creative writing course can help you to access your creativity. One useful technique is that of 'free-writing', where you just get up in the morning and begin, straightaway, to write about your dreams and feelings. You write completely non-judgementally, as a stream of consciousness, and then review the themes and ideas at different times. Other techniques include sensory aware-ness, where you feel something in your hands with your eyes closed – an egg or a grape, say, and then write about everything it evokes. Or try a memory exercise where you remember a place that inspired strong feelings, and write about it.

All of these techniques help us to use what Edward de Bono (see page 227) calls 'creative pause'. That is, we take a moment or two just to stop and absorb what is happening around us. We are only able to notice sensory experiences when we take the time to pause. And we can take this tech-nique further by focusing on something very specific that we notice: the colour of the light, perhaps, or the back-ground hum of the city.

Now move these ideas to apply to creativity at work – let's say you want to bring more creativity to your presen-tations. You decide to take a 'creative pause' by getting off the roller coaster of delivering the same presentation time after time. Give yourself a month off. During this month you will focus intently on one theme: how do people make your subject matter really impactful? You find your-self getting ideas from all sorts of sources: radio shows, books, adverts, children playing in the park and, more obviously, other people's presentations. You've stopped and you've focused. As a result, the world is throwing up ideas to you.

Have you had experience of this? Many people have. You have a question in the front of your mind and then you notice – in all sorts of unexpected contexts – ideas that are relevant to this question. This is testimony to the power of our individual perception: and it's also the key to invention and creativity.

We've already established that structure is an important part of creativity; but how do we free up fixed patterns of ideas that may be inhibiting us? Well, mind-mapping, popularised by Tony Buzan is one way of doing this. You take a central idea and then freefall in your thinking about all the images, abstracts, thoughts and associations that could spring out this idea. Here's an example:

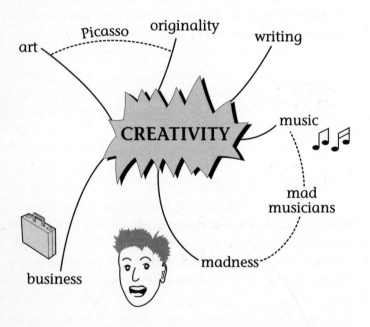

Now a more linear approach to subject would go like this:

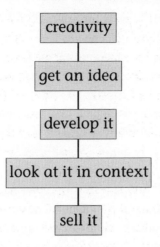

Another useful approach is to take multiple perspectives – in other words, taking several different viewpoints of your subject. The following is a good example:

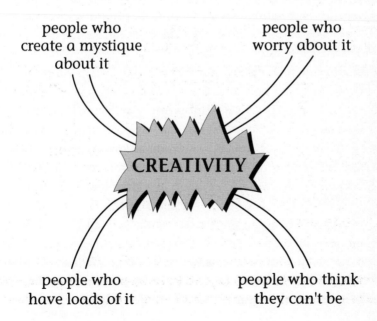

I can't emphasise enough how helpful it is to draw or to illustrate the whole picture. To be more creative about it you are going to make some unexpected connections and you can only do this if the whole territory is in front of you.

Mind-mapping stimulates our creativity through activating parts of the brain that seem to be sluggish. Specific areas of our brains handle reasoning, linear thinking and analysis, and for many of us, they are the parts that get the most exercise. The areas that handle imagination, visualisation and divergent leaps of connection may not be nearly so fit. A technique like mind-mapping pulls these parts into action.

Ask challenging questions. This is where creative people cause trouble. Questions like 'Although we've been doing it this way for years, is this really the best way of doing it?' or repeatedly asking 'Why?' about an approach are a good way to find better ways of doing it. Adopting multiple perspectives about values behind actions can also be helpful – something along the lines of 'OK, if profit wasn't the main value behind this approach, but high quality instead, how would we do things differently?' Challenging central ideas, assumptions and limitations within which you operate can generate new insights.

Playing wild-word and idea-association games can also free up creative thinking. So take our idea of 'impactful presentations' and an association of a victorious boxer (not that I approve of the sport, you understand). Linking these two ideas you get short rounds, bells ringing, loads of movement, lots of punching, bursts of high energy punctuated with moments of respite. Why not make your presentation shorter, punctuated with audience involvement every five minutes or so, keep it high energy and leave them wanting more? (But *please* don't decide to make a grand entrance to Tina Turner singing 'You're Simply The Best'. That would be an image too far!)

Go to Paris. No, all this creative talk has *not* made me go bananas. It's just that unlike London, which is a city dominated by commerce, creativity takes precedence in Paris. There is wonderful art everywhere, the food is fab, the people look terrific and buying from a chi-chi boutique is a joyously sensual experience, as your purchases are wrapped with great care and attention to detail. Of course, Paris isn't the only place like this – I've heard that Barcelona is inspiring, too – but the point is simply to put yourself into a new stimulating environment, even if it's just for a day trip. New stimuli and a different way of doing things can really help you look afresh at what you are doing.

Expressing creativity goes to the core of motivation. We make something, feel a great sense of achievement about it, and want to make it again, or to make it bigger, better or differently. Any entrepreneurial activity is based on creating something. When we create, we involve ourselves in something that is bigger than all of our problems, and little grinding day-to-day concerns. People working together on a creative enterprise, when thoroughly engaged, forget all their little personality differences and irritations with one another. The creation transcends them. Living creatively is a guarantee that you will feel motivated, and I hope this chapter has given you some ideas about how to do this more fully.

5 *Coping with Crisis*

'That which does not kill me makes me stronger.'
Nietzsche

In a crisis, American author, Dr Bernie Siegel asks himself, 'What would Lassie do here?'; writer India Knight asks herself, 'What would Madonna do here?'; and I ask myself, 'What would Hillary Clinton do here?' Now this is not because I identify with Hillary in any special way; in fact, I'm more likely to feel to the contrary. However, I speculate about her perspective because I know it's likely to be very different to my own rather soppy inclinations. Hillary categorically does not do soppiness.

I'm aware that this is a slightly light-hearted approach to a potentially serious chapter, but one of the main messages of this chapter is that a sense of humour helps to maintain a sense of perspective. One of the most momentous things that happened to me was the death of my father. I loved him very much and he'd had cancer. The morning of his death the house was full of aweeping and awailing Welsh relatives and we were awash with Bara Brith, the fruit loaf we Welsh traditionally give to one another in times of need. I put on the kettle and went in to see my mother, who was in mourning with relatives in the darkened front room. 'Mum, would you like a coffin?' I said, meaning to offer coffee. There was a moment's horrified pause, then everyone burst out laughing. We all felt a bit better after that, and my dad would have laughed, too.

So in this chapter, and without too much doom and

gloom, I hope, I'm going to look at how we react during a crisis, and how to remotivate ourselves afterwards.

Crisis reactions

Someone who once worked for me loved crisis.

One day I came downstairs for a break and she said, 'Sit down, I've got some bad news.' I did as I was told, adopting a grave air of expectation. 'John Lewis can't deliver your sofa until next week,' she said. I gasped. Only the gasp was not the response she thought it was. It was a gasp of incredulity that anyone could believe that a delayed sofa delivery was worthy of this drama. You'll have encountered this type of person, too, I'm sure – drama queens of both sexes who are constantly looking for excitement to pep up their beige little lives.

And this illustrates an important point about crisis. Our definition of a 'crisis' really depends on how we see things as individuals. Today – and particularly because of successful litigation leading to compensation – we have a flourishing stress industry. But the word is confusing. Is 'stress' the cause of our response, something in the ether, attacking us from all sides, or does 'stress' describe our response, the cracking-up we experience? Hans Seyle, an early and hugely influential stress researcher, revealed that, in hindsight, he wished he'd never used the word 'stress' to describe response to pressure. He felt that 'strain' was far more accurate. And it can be very difficult to trace the response an individual is experiencing back to its true root cause. Many people who claim to be stressed at work, for instance, will be experiencing strain in other areas of their lives, too.

I don't want to sound unsympathetic, but stress is used

in many woolly contexts today. Undoubtedly there are some triggers that would cause the great majority of us to feel under strain: bereavement, serious illness, redundancy, divorce and separation. But then again, not always – sometimes the death of a parent or spouse, or a divorce, can be positively liberating. On the other hand, a very genuine reaction can sometimes occur in an individual who perceives themselves in a state of crisis, where no one else can see it. Take Deirdre, for example:

> Deidre was professionally successful and in a long-term happy relationship. She felt fulfilled as a grandmother – her daughter Kim lived with her boyfriend and they had a toddler. Deidre had never liked Kim's boyfriend, Greg, but tolerated him for Kim's sake. Twenty-five years previously, when Deidre had become a mother herself, she was abandoned by her husband Tom when Kim was six months old. They had never seen him again and Deidre had rebuilt her life.
>
> Kim phones Deidre to tell her that she and Greg are splitting up. On the surface Deidre has mixed feelings, concern about her daughter and granddaughter, but also relief that Greg is leaving. Everyone she tells about it comments, 'Well, you never liked him anyway.' But deep inside Deidre feels like she is having a crisis. All of the feelings of panic and abandonment that she felt when Tom left still seem to be there and she feels guilty about him leaving, that it was in some way her fault. Now Kim is to be abandoned again. Deidre gets depressed and seeks help from her GP, who suggests therapy and anti-depressants. She recovers eventually, though still few of her friends and relatives understand why she had the crisis.

Reaction chain

When a crisis occurs, the psychological reactions are usually as follows: the crisis strikes and we attack something or someone, and/or feel numb. Then we get upset. This is where some people get stuck; they notice that perhaps they get attention and care while being upset and so they stay that way. They play the victim and sometimes they continue to do so for the rest of their lives. The rest of us find various ways of coping and eventually recover and go on to thrive.

Human beings are generally very resilient. During research for this book, I discovered that a tenth of children with psychotic parents appear to be completely unscathed by the experience. Of sexual-abuse victims, over half will be able to resume normal sex lives, often with help of therapy. Individuals like Simon Weston – the soldier who was horribly burnt in the Falklands War and now runs his own charity – are wonderful examples of resilience. The extent to which our will to thrive can help us overcome bad experiences and get on with life is nothing less than extraordinary. With the exception of those of us on a bottle of vodka and forty Silk Cut a day, we want to survive.

Contradictions in people

One of my favourite theories about human beings is called 'personal construct psychology'. Those of you who have read my previous book, *Irresistibility: Secrets of selling yourself*, will be familiar with this theme. What this theory says is that all of us have constructs or filters, with opposing or contrasting ideas at either end of them, through which we make meaning of everything that happens to us. For instance, I might have an intellectual uneducated construct which I'm fond of using, especially to judge people. When I meet you and you happen to have a PhD from Harvard, you'll understand why I'm finding you so instantly impressive.

Construct ideas provide us with a useful way of understanding what happens to us during a crisis. Let's say something truly dreadful happens, and you lose several members of your family in a Lockerbie-type disaster. Your constructs are likely to include ideas like love/hate, loss/gain, family/friends, relationships/enmities, closeness/distance, sense of belonging/isolation, and being looked after/being abandoned. You can gather from this list that these would take a mighty irreversible battering with the news that your close relatives had perished in such circumstances. Your whole map of where you were in life would be destroyed. To come out the other end of such a crisis, you would need to create some significant new constructs for yourself, which would probably include such ideas as acceptance/rejection, future orientated/past orientated, close friends/isolation.

Where you feel generally that you do not cope with crisis very well, then it can be useful to choose three crises from your life and to ask yourself what were the most important constructs that got rocked or destroyed during those times. Often when people do this exercise they find that themes emerge because the constructs have common ideas: perhaps they repeatedly feel hugely out of control during crisis or a great sense that what was happening was unfair.

This is what Katherine, a mother, told me:

> *My dad died when I was about nine and I think that was the first crisis I really experienced. We were three children and my mum had a real hard time bringing us up, though she was sustained by strong religious faith. Whenever I think of crisis it is do with change and a great fear I have of losing people and aspects of my life. I don't think I cope as well as most people with things like moving and changing jobs. What I do now to help me is that I list everything that I might lose during a change and ask myself whether any of these losses might actually be beneficial. Then I list all the good things that change will bring us and ask myself how I can make the most of these. To counteract my natural tendency to dwell on the downside, I give myself about fifteen minutes a day, where I restrict myself to thinking about and visualising the good aspects of the change. I often do this just before the kids come home from school and it really gives me a bit of a boost. I don't think I'll ever be someone who loves change – but at least I'm keeping the worst demons at bay.*

Deliberately focusing on the upside of a situation, while not denying that the downside exists, can help increase a general sense of optimism.

Helpful contradictions

These contradictions within us, which I describe as constructs, are not usually purely 'either/or' states, but also 'both/and'. Let me take a favourite example. You meet someone who, within five minutes of being in their company, sends your stomach churning and you start to have a strong 'Oh no' message in your head. You meet this person several times over the subsequent months, always in a work context, and you find that you think about them rather a lot. Some of their behaviour you really object to, and dislike intensely, at other times you find them absolutely riveting and compelling. You seem to be incapable of anything other than strong reactions to this person. Yes, you've guessed it, you're in *luuurrvve*.

And this is about experiencing attraction and repulsion, not really on an either/or basis, though it may feel like that at different times, but holding both contradictory reactions for the same person. Very often these feelings I've described are also accompanied by an 'I'm extremely similar to him'/'he is completely alien to me' construct as well, again both ideas being held together.

Studies of what makes for good leadership often identify 'tolerance of ambiguity' as a key aspect. That means being able to understand and accept that we can all hold ideas that seem to be irreconcilably opposite to one another, and yet these ideas can be held mutually. You could call this dichotomy, paradox, or dialectic – whichever you fancy.

And studies of hardy individuals who cope admirably with crisis show that they are able to hold specific pairs of psychological contradictions, demonstrating two seemingly very different qualities. They are:

Consideration for others/selfishness: We might think that gung-ho Bruce Willis types would cope very well with crisis, but studies of military performance show this not to be the case. Top 'copers' do think of other people and their responses, realising just how much we have in common with one another. Because of this orientation, they are able to make decisions for the general good, quickly. But these individuals are also able to prioritise quickly what is necessary for their own survival, paying especial attention to looking after themselves when the going is tough.

This idea is clarified in Nicola's story:

> *Just after we had our third child, my partner Richard was made redundant. I was desperately tired and we both seemed to be ill all the time, with one minor complaint after another. I rather shocked other members of the family by making my fitness a top priority, going as far as investing in personal training. I just felt I had to feel as fit as I could to keep cheerful and resilient for everyone. It definitely was a good idea, though I suspect that behind my back there were mutterings about 'selfish' and 'taken leave of her senses'.*

When Nicola looked back after this time, she really felt that looking after herself had helped her to look after others, and to take the best decisions.

Empathy / toughness: If you think of a top crisis negotiator, these two qualities spring to mind. Empathy to understand why others are behaving as they are is vital: it's the best way of predicting how others will respond in a crisis. But empathy must be contained by toughness; if it's not, you'll have no means of deciding upon and pressurising people into action. Toughness means that you see the requirements of the situation as well as understanding the emotions involved. When tough decisions need to be taken, they will be taken in the light of their effect on others' emotions.

Proactivity / acquiescence: I'm sure you've experienced a person who *doesn't* hold this balanced construct; they are particularly useless in a crisis. They will often regard themselves as being a hugely proactive self-starter who constantly takes initiatives. The trouble is that they are unable to stop themselves from being constantly 'busy', and when a crisis arises, they respond with manic activity and panic. They lack the ability to stop, reflect, see what is working, go along with it, and simply be proactive about the issue or activity that really could use some of their famous momentum. When you feel that you are living your life from crisis to crisis, perhaps you could benefit from putting yourself temporarily into a state of acquiescence. Just go with the flow for a while, as Zen philosophers suggest.

Self-confidence/self-monitoring: Great 'copers' are confident about their ability to handle what life throws at them, but not so confident that they become dangerously arrogant. They will notice their responses to things, how well they are performing and how close they are to achieving what they want in a crisis. They will feel good about themselves and in a crisis use positive self-talk to keep boosting their own and other people's motivation. This is not the same as seeing everything in a positive light – indeed, this can be dangerous in a crisis, as you need a degree of pessimism to watch out for anything else that could go wrong. Positive talk is not a means of denying the true reality of the situation, it's just a means of encouraging further use of helpful behaviour.

Dorian, a businessman, recalled a past crisis:

A few years ago, a lot went wrong in my life. My father died unexpectedly, my health was poor and my business was hit by recession. I'm naturally quite pessimistic at work anyway; my business is high-risk and I always need to think about the drawbacks of schemes. I knew I could cope with things, but I

> *was far more flexible that usual about what I tackled every*
> *day. If I felt exhausted, I did only the necessary minimum.*
> *And each evening I made myself think about what had gone*
> *well that day, and congratulated myself on surviving it.*

Coping practically in a crisis

The golden rule in any crisis situation is 'Don't panic'.
Breathe slowly and deeply, letting the air drop low into
your lungs; stand or sit in a firm position so that your body
literally feels supported. Slow yourself down and pull yourself back from the situation, as if you are pausing to survey
it. It is very important to stay calm because when we
become very emotional, we become much more accident
prone. For example, insurance companies know this from
the figures showing a correlation between people who are
going through divorces or separations and car accidents.
When we panic, our sympathetic nervous system takes
over and we may start to feel a 'fight or flight' response,
where we become aggressive or fearful.

You will want to quickly absorb as much information as
you can about the situation and expect to do something to
be able to influence it. Is there any action you can take
to improve the situation? Sometimes the only influence we
can exert is on our own responses, and or to help other
people with theirs. It often helps to think of all the possible
actions and reactions that could be available. When my
partner was taken seriously ill last year, there was some joy
that we would have him home more, even though the
overriding response was one of concern for his health.

I'm sure you are aware that knowledge helps in a crisis,
and a good general knowledge about first aid, safety

procedures, and emotional responses is always useful.
You're almost certainly aware, too, that doctors, pilots and
the emergency services endlessly rehearse disaster scenarios.
They are trained so that they can perform their sequence
of actions in the midst of complete chaos. We may not have
their luxury of foresight, but developing the skills to cope
well with smaller incidents, certainly prepares us for crisis.

The same approach applies to a crisis situation that does
not actually involve a physical trauma. While stressful situations cannot always be anticipated, we can adopt a sort
of 'prepared for anything' mentality, in which we mentally
rehearse how we will cope with problems that arise. Again,
self-awareness is the key here. If you know that you react
in a certain way to stressful situations, practise walking
yourself through some sample scenarios that you may have
encountered in the past, or perhaps anticipate in the future.
Think about how you would react, and visualise yourself
taking a step back, pausing, collecting your thoughts, and
moving forward in a positive way. Consider the various
options you have to address the situation, and visualise
yourself putting them into action. Continually remind
yourself that you have the resources to cope, and that you
are strong enough to see things through. In the end, if
you are prepared for the worst, and find a method of
coping with that scenario, the reality of any stressful situation will be, well, that much less stressful.

There is a certain sort of communication that works
best in a crisis. It's best to keep messages short and to the
point, with a calm delivery. Give people clear directions,
evaluate what's happening and let people know the upside
of any directions you give them. Lots of repetition may be
necessary, because under pressure our listening skills
become less effective.

The more time we spend in a state of 'engaged relaxation' – where our attention is one hundred per cent focused on the present and what is happening in our environment, but we are also fairly relaxed – the better we will cope with a crisis. If you are not very familiar with this state, then you will find it helpful to practise it. Think of yourself as a researcher trawling different environments for greater understanding of what is really going on; use exercise, meditation, good sleep and eating habits, and taking time for yourself to improve relaxation. You will cope better if you give yourself a break during stressful times, and in less demanding periods, you can take the opportunity to build yourself up so that you are physically and emotionally able to cope with whatever life throws at you.

When a crisis seems to last a long time – in the case of recovering from bereavement, coping with serious illness, or going through a messy divorce – then it's very helpful not to become too judgmental, and to take things step by step, living life day by day. When asked about clumsy comments people made about her terminally-ill husband, writer John Diamond, journalist and cookery writer Nigella Lawson said that she always tried to see the intention behind the comment, rather than the comment itself. If you start to be too judgmental, your critical thinking will get in the way of your intuition, which you need at this time. It is your intuitive powers that will help you to see opportunities and positive routes for change.

Remotivating yourself

Here are lots of ideas for remotivating yourself during and after a crisis, some serious, some light-hearted, all for the trying:

Express your emotions. You will benefit from getting out whatever you feel about the situation, even if it's just a good cry in private. Some people find writing down their emotional responses very helpful and research seems to suggest this is most beneficial for recovery. If emoting's not your style, it is still important for you to acknowledge and identify the emotions that you are feeling, rather than letting them churn chaotically inside you.

Give boundaries to your negativity. If you are in a long-term crisis and you really have no idea how things will pan out, you may experience a lot of very negative feelings. But give yourself boundaries to their expression. Allow yourself a miserable hour once a day, or let yourself stay miserable till four o'clock in the afternoon and then resolve to change mood with tea and a bun.

Nicky is a teacher:

> When I was diagnosed with breast cancer, I gave myself a 'worrying hour'. I chose the time of day where I felt strongest, just after breakfast, and I resolved to fret furiously then. Sometimes I didn't manage to fill the whole hour, and other times the worry would keep creeping back later in the day. But I did find that knowing I had this time made it much easier for me to get on with my life for the rest of the day.

When your negative feelings become completely uncontrollable, then get thee to thy doctor.

Don't be too good or too nice: Going round martyring ourselves and suffering silently will harm us eventually. Much better to get used to expressing our negative feelings about what is going on. Get a confidante to whom you can really open up and who listens non-judgmentally.

You may well be thinking here 'Yes, but you're a psychologist, all your mates are likely to do that', and you'd have a point. But if you explain to someone close that you feel bad about what is going on and you'd like to talk about it, they will at least be forewarned. Explain that you do not want advice, just to air the resentment or anger you're feeling.

Your partner may be a good choice for this, provided they are not too upset by what is going on. In which case, you will find it more useful to talk to someone who is at some distance from the crisis. There are very few people who will not respond to – and, indeed, rise to – a genuine cry for help.

Reflect on the experience. Playing the experience in your mind's eye, with yourself almost as an observer can be helpful. You might even want to fade the experience into the distance to help put in behind you; or, indeed, literally to see it going behind you and receding into infinity. This is the disaster movie where you get to call the concluding shots. When you are doing this, you want to feel as neutral as possible about it; don't rationalise what happened, or justify or criticise your actions.

Describe what happened. We can talk things out of our system and it is a good idea to relay the experience to a sympathetic listener as soon as you feel you can after a crisis. If we relay it enough times to enough people, we might just about get exhausted with the whole thing and forget it. Except we all know women, and there seem to be a lot of them around, who endlessly retell their birth experiences, whether the rest of us what to know about their episiotomies or not . . .

Identify learning. If there's anything you've learnt from the experience, then clarify exactly what that is and how you would do things differently next time – if there could be one.

Distract yourself. Seek out the frivolous and fun as distraction. Make-up and chocolate are my relatively harmless antidotes to worrying about quite serious things. Get a sense of playfulness about life; flirt with people, spend time playing with kids, go ten-pin bowling, bungy jumping, paintballing or spa-visiting. Take pleasure in small everyday pleasures – the perfect cappuccino, *Hello* and *OK* magazines, the absorbing radio play, deliciously painted toe nails, or a perfect present for someone. Enjoy the little things.

Get awestruck. There's a new form of therapy I've invented and it's called 'insignificance therapy'. However bad we are feeling, there are places we can go to where we become awestruck by the amazing beauty of nature or the genius of individuals. I recommend Rhossili beach in the Gower, South Wales, for the first and the Picasso Museum in Paris for the second. This therapy works for those of us recovering from a crisis, or those of us who are suffering from hubris, the sense that we are much more significant than we really are.

Throw yourself into an absorbing project. So you may have lost your partner or your job, but you can still embark on a total redesign of your garden, or mastering diesel-engine maintenance. A project slightly tangential to the rest of your life may be a great way of restoring your morale.

Give yourself the occasional affirmation. Make sure that you comment favourably on your progress when you feel it's due. If you try to brainwash yourself through constant affirmation of the 'every day I get stronger and stronger' variety, you may find that your imagination goes into battle with your will and your imagination may win.

Believe in God and have no reverence. We're back here to another one of those contradictions or paradoxes in which we human beings seem to revel. Studies of long-term AIDS survivors show that they often have both a spiritual side and also a great capacity for irreverence. Other studies show that people who have spiritual or religious beliefs are generally happier than the rest of us.

Although these ideas sound contradictory – holding religious or spiritual beliefs while being irreverent, there is one core idea here. It's the sense that we are all very strongly connected with one another, and that no single idea or person should be elevated to the extent that they take themselves too seriously. We're talking those kitsch pictures of Jesus in a day-glo kaftan surrounded by podgy cherubs, really. Immensely cheering.

Have faith in the future. More seriously, Victor Frankl, who was a concentration camp survivor and wrote about life in the camps, described the people who survived as having faith in the future. This was clearly a characteristic that kept people going and fighting for their lives.

Exercise your imagination. The greatest potential you have to remotivate yourself lies in your capacity to visualise how things might be different. See the crisis resolved in the way that you would like it, see yourself strengthened as a result of it. How will you look, sound and feel? How will others be responding to you? When you're finding the going tough, just take a little mental trip to the Maldives, or New York or the Cotswolds – and see yourself having a good time there – to give yourself a break from the angst.

Look after your attention. Our attention is not something that gets mentioned much in the run-of-the-mill of things. During and after a crisis, though, it can be helpful to think about it as a part of you that needs special consideration.

Let's say that you or your partner are quite ill and your attention is spent much of the time on medical matters. Or you've lost your job and your attention is going into searching for a job most of the time. Then give it the break it deserves: take it to a funny movie, a bookshop, a make-up emporium or a football match. When we've been through a tough time, our attention may need a bit of a break, before we get it focusing on where we go next. We can help and control our attention through practising skills of concentration, absorption and distraction.

Study inspiring people. Talk to people with interesting stories who have survived crisis or just thrive on challenge. They are everywhere. I have a neighbour in my sleepy Welsh town who has just taken up parachute jumping. She is eighty-one. There are lots of books around that contain inspiring stories. My favourites, unbeatable for black humour, irreverence and wit are journalist John Diamond's *Only Cowards Get Cancer*, and Ruth Picardie's *Before I Say Goodbye*.

Sometimes, a crisis can leave us feeling that our lives will never be the same again, and that we want to change direction, dramatically. If this is the case, this next chapter will help you to do just that.

6 *This is your Calling Calling*

> '*If you do not get it from yourself, then where will you go for it?*'
> The Buddha

Oh, life used to be so simple, didn't it? You'd be born into a family with a clear sense of its place in society. You'd be destined to become a governess or a gamekeeper or a lady or lord of the manor. Your path would be charted, and only through a great stroke of luck or misfortune would your future turn out to be any different than expected. Nowadays it's all a lot less predictable and a lot tougher. You can be born into obscure ordinariness and people expect you to become Madonna or Maradona or Kulfi Annan. If you're the slightest bit ambitious, then people think there are no limits to what you can achieve. We are talking *pressure to perform* here, baby.

This is your drive calling

If you are ambitious, and you haven't found the right direction yet, you will probably have bouts of restlessness, frustration, fantasy trips and fatigue. You will want to succeed desperately – and be mad that you don't know how. You'll alternate between feeling wildly motivated and utterly hopeless. You will feel a great sense of drive, but you won't know where to take it.

Drive makes us want to achieve things and to make an impact on the world. We can feel guilty for experiencing it. Ideas like 'How dare little me from my humble background aspire that high', 'How can someone who's got two small kids dream of doing that' or 'What you're hoping to do is completely unrealistic' can make us feel bad. As we discussed in Chapter Four, other people may envy our drive and want to make us feel bad about it.

Cally describes her experience:

> I always wanted to be a designer – my dad and mum were supervisors in a clothing factory in the Midlands. The other kids at school used to ridicule me; I was always drawing and dressing in outlandish clothes. I think some of my family found me embarrassing. When I got eventually got in to design school in London, the same people were shocked, and when I went to work in Paris, they couldn't believe it. But my aim to be a designer was always stronger than the sniping. I can't help smirking when I go back and meet those people now – especially as they all know I work for a couture house.

No book on motivation can give you drive, nor can any other person. You've either got it or you haven't. Drive is ambition, really; it's the desire to make something of yourself and your life. I never believe celebrities who have clearly chosen and worked to become stars, while saying things like: 'I'm really very lazy' or 'I'm not at all ambitious'. I suspect that this is just a sentiment they think will make them more popular with the public. Or perhaps it implies that they are so brilliant they've got where they are without really trying. After all, there are all sorts of other legal ways of making loads of cash that don't require you to wear a disguise to the supermarket.

Make no bones about it, as long as it's not hurting you or anyone else, drive is a great attribute. But it's much easier to deal with if you are clear about direction. That's what we look at in this chapter – clarifying where you are meant to be going in life. In other words, we'll look at ways to find and exploit your calling. We look at who you are, what you're really good at, what's important to you, and how you turn your calling into a reality.

Your defining moments

When I first left university, I acted for a few years. An actress I knew had become an agent. She came to see me in a play that later transferred to London's West End. 'Daaahling,' she said to me after the show, 'you were so gauche.' While this was hurtful, it made me resolve to conquer this gaucheness, or at least use it to be funny. To some extent I must have succeeded, as recent feed-back from a conference speech I gave described me as 'psychology's answer to Billy Connolly'. Without the beard, you understand.

This was an odd defining moment, but I remember it vividly. If you were telling the story of your life, what would be the defining moments or turning points? They may not be the obvious things, like births, deaths and marriages. What has occurred in your life to make you take powerful decisions? And what were these decisions about? What were the feelings behind them? Have these feelings resurfaced several times? What personal qualities do they represent?

People have told me their defining moments have been about such diverse themes as succeeding with others to produce something, overwhelming feelings of love, winning against all the odds, healing something or someone. Take Gerry, for example; he's a doctor:

> *When I was about eight or nine, there was a bird with a damaged wing in our garden. My mum and I got it better; we looked after it and fed it until it could fly again. I just remember the most incredible feeling of satisfaction when I saw that bird taking off into the air. I'm pretty sure it contributed to what I've ended up doing.*

In my case, my agent friend's comments created in me a strong resolve to prove that her condemnation of me was wrong. It was irrelevant that her viewpoint might have been isolated. Her hurtfulness acted as a catalyst for me to learn about the impact we make on one another. In a way, she gave me a new career.

Confusing times

A history e-zine of the future may well describe recent times in this way:

> *The end of the twentieth century was a period where, in the West, traditional institutions like the church, the government and the law lost significance. Instead, two forces, IT and individualism, became very important. People started to work differently – from home and on the move – and they no longer expected their employers to look after them for life. The climate for business and growth was entrepreneurial and exciting. Fewer people married, more people lived by themselves and women put off child-bearing until early middle age. As for morality, the royals and politicians were seen as representative of a marked decline.*
>
> *Small wonder that at the beginning of the twenty-first century lots of us appeared to be experiencing something of an identity crisis. To help us, we became fixated with*

celebrities – the most successful of whom, like Madonna,
constantly reinvented themselves, maintaining the publicity
that is their oxygen. Some of these celebrities possessed
questionable talent, but they were pushy and persistent
enough to be featured in the international press regularly.
   The other social phenomenon that helped was the
docusoap. Real-life people wrestled with real-life situations
– at least, that is what the television companies would have
us believe – in airports, on remote islands or in 'Big Brother'
set-ups. And these people's problems made the viewers feel
a bit better about their own uncertainties.
   The other thing people to did to clarify identity was shop.

Now all this change, 'churn' or 'permanent whitewater', as it's been called, creates a hugely vital environment. No matter where you are coming from, there is lots of opportunity and potential to reinvent yourself successfully, largely through getting the image right. It's a climate that offers potential for the entrepreneurial and the confident to become successful very quickly.

But the downside is that lots of us don't know who we are. We help to clarify our images through what we consume. For example, my Boden catalogue reiterates my self-image of a home-loving mother who lives by the sea but still wants to wear funky clothes. But, often, that's not enough. The quick-fix of identity that consumption gives us is over pretty quickly – either we have to have endless money to continue consuming relentlessly or we're left with that feeling of 'Well, after the initial euphoria of wearing this new cardie, I still don't know who I am'.

It's hardly coincidence – is it? – that the most consumer-driven society (America) also has a very large number of people engaged in tracing their family trees. Presumably it gives them some deeper roots, and a clearer sense of their own identity.

A mind to creation

Some of us will have religious beliefs that give us great comfort. We believe that there is a purpose and plan behind things that happen – and that our fate is guided by a higher prescience as part of the plan. Chaos theory creates the idea that there is very little that can be controlled and predicted in life, but that the universe goes through periods of great turbulence and chaos alternating with quieter, more orderly periods where patterns may emerge. Post-modern thinking emphasises the subjective – that we are all caught up in networks of power, that none of us is free – and that everything is about interpretation. And different theories about human beings will explain our sense of purpose. Recently, for instance, there have been a rash of books published by evolutionary psychologists empha-sising 'selfish genes', which suggests that much of what we do will be motivated by our genes surviving and perpetuating themselves.

Whether we believe there is a big purpose behind life or not, when we want to be able to motivate ourselves and others, we need a clear sense of purpose about our lives.

Finding your essence

When I look at babies I see innocence and beauty. Yes, they want to be fed, allowed to sleep, and cuddled and cosseted. But, alongside the self-interest, there is goodness, too, and a huge desire to connect with other human beings. And this desire often develops into altruism, the desire to live peaceably with others, and to derive enormous satisfaction from helping others. In essence, we have both good and bad qualities.

Essential you exercises

Write a description of yourself through the eyes of three of your friends: Why are you their friend? What are your best qualities? What have you done to demonstrate these qualities?

Now write your autobiography. It doesn't have to be very long, but give yourself the luxury of an hour off to do it. Review it over the next few days, and examine it for themes. How have you changed? What are your best experiences? What do you like to avoid and when do you do it? What matters to you most, and how have things shifted in importance over the years? What do you still hold dearest to your heart? What do you get from work and how does it measure up to your expectations or aspirations?

Next, get yourself into a relaxed state, lying on the bed or the floor, if it's comfortable enough. Breathe slowly and easily into the bottom of your lungs and let your mind drift. If you find it difficult to settle, mentally create a visual image of one small shape – a circle, square or triangle of light within complete darkness. Just focus on that image till you feel more settled. Now just start to fantasise about yourself as a god or goddess. What quality would you represent? What would you do in the world? What would people worship you for? (Confession time: during tough times, and in a bout of confusion, I have signed off e-mails as Philippa, Warrior Queen of South Glamorgan. Stick that in your corporate in-tray!)

Dig out some photos of you as a child. Do certain qualities repeatedly shine through in these photos? Has this quality come through at other times in your life? When I do this exercise I repeatedly see a slightly quizzical expression on my face. I remain quizzical, doing both formal and informal research about life. Where you see a distinctive quality repeated, think about whether you are content with that quality, or whether you would like to convey something different.

Think about what you wanted to do as a child. Has it changed? If so, what put you off the path you had envisioned or chosen for yourself?

Ask someone whose opinion you really trust what their very first impression of you was. The psychologist Eric Berne thought that when we first meet people the part of us that is still 'child' meets their 'child'. What was their impression of your 'child'? What did they see that they liked?

What feedback do you get from other people about 'who you are'? Maria was starting a post-graduate course many years after graduating. The method of study involved a great deal of group debate, led by professors. 'Blimey,' one of her closest friends said, 'they'll find you a challenge.' Several weeks later, Maria announced her intention to apply to join a public body related to the health service, something she knew a lot about. 'Blimey,' her husband said, 'those civil servants will find you a handful; they won't know how to cope.' She started to wonder whether she was in danger of being too forceful . . . She resolved to tone down her behaviour in certain situations, to appear more of a diplomat.

If you had the opportunity to take a year off, what would you do? How would you feel?

In the previous chapter, I mentioned the idea of constructs; opposing pairs of themes or ideas that we all hold in our minds. We can sometimes find that the way others perceive us is opposite to the impression we hold of ourselves. We work hard to convey the opposite qualities to those that we dislike in ourselves: so the truly shy person is arrogant and opinionated to others; the workaholic conveys the impression of being totally laid back; the intellectual acts as a lad or a ladette.

Your calling can take its time . . .

We have a mad educational system. By eighteen we're supposed to have a pretty clear idea about what we want to study at college. By twenty-one we're supposed to be ready to enter the job market. Hey Presto! Off we go on our career track. Sadly, life ain't really like that . . . Alan is forty-two, and this is his experience:

> *I went to university to do business studies, because I couldn't think of anything else I wanted to do and it seemed like a respectable, responsible choice. I loved university life and got on to the social committee organising gigs in the students' union. I scraped a third. After university, I dabbled in journalism for a while, then public relations, and in my late twenties started running venues and promoting gigs. I'm semi-retired now. It wasn't just a hugely fulfilling role, but a very lucrative one too.*

Alan eventually returned to what he loved doing as a student – and turned it into a successful career.

An awful lot of interesting people that I know have 'pottered' during their twenties. They've been pottering around different partners, places to live, jobs and interests.

It's only in their late twenties or early thirties that they've felt certain enough to set direction. And why not? Provided their 'pottering' has not bankrupted them or their family, been hugely illegal or hurt others, it's pretty useful.

Your calling will probably have sent indicators

The other day I was talking with my friend Nigel – who I've known nearly all my life – about our first meeting. He was eight and I was six. We both attended Tabernacle Baptist Chapel where, on Sundays, you were expected to do a turn in the pulpit at morning service. We children were given badges following these turns. 'I can still picture you now,' said Nigel, 'extremely rotund coming out of the service looking very pleased with yourself. All the other children just wore their one badge for that morning's efforts. But your chest was covered with about thirty badges, because you insisted – every Sunday – that you wore your entire collection.' I still find it very hard to throw out approving feedback sheets from workshops.

I read drama for my first degree at university, but, while I was there, I co-edited the university newspaper. For seven years after university I wrote nothing at all. Then, then in my late twenties, I met someone who got me a publishing deal . . .

Rather like chaos theory says, patterns do emerge during periods of calm and order in between bouts of turbulence.

Your calling is deeply internal

When I train politicians and business people, I often need to ask them awkward questions. One of the most awkward questions is: 'What is your purpose?' And it often needs to be qualified with: 'Why are you here on the planet?' People are often embarrassed and flustered by this approach; It needs practice and application to become comfortable with inward journeys and self-analysis. Sometimes people lack direction because of insufficient practice at dialoguing with their inner being:

Hallo in there! exercises

Meditation is easy to learn. Make sure that you won't be interrupted and that you are warm enough to stay comfortable for 10 to 20 minutes. Get yourself in a relaxed position on the floor. (I use a backstretcher, which is a kind of wooden grill that gives you mild traction, to lie on. And no, this isn't some kind of masochistic fetish – it stretches out the neck and back muscles while I meditate. It's highly recommended if you do a lot of computer work). Close your eyes and place a hand lightly on your stomach. Be aware of your breath dropping low into the body and the stomach rising, then the stomach flattening as the breath leaves. Breathe easily and slowly. Every time your breath leaves, feel tension slip away. As thoughts come into your mind, let them drift through. Observe them and let them slip away. You are almost outside of your thinking, just watching your ideas. Suspend judgement on your thoughts; simply notice that they are occurring. Relax. When you feel pleasantly rested, get up gently and gradually. You should feel greatly refreshed. It's undoubtedly easier to meditate at some points of the day than others. First thing in the morning, after three espressos, is probably not the ideal time . . .

Once you get into a meditative state, you can control your thoughts constructively. Let's say you want to meditate yourself into a clearer direction. A visualisation exercise will help here. Create two characters. One is your protector – a wise woman or man who wants the very best for you, but who also has a conscience about the results of your actions on others. She is your protector and nurturer. Get her to observe you and your life and offer advice about what you could do next. Any self-defeating thoughts can be represented by an ugly little gremlin, who your protector swipes with her magic wand, should he pipe up or start to come near.

If meditation is not for you, a long walk or outing that allows you to commune with nature and just spend time alone with your thoughts can be beneficial.

Your calling emerges in action

One of the ways in which human beings respond to stress is through the fight, flight or freeze response. When we're confused and unclear about our direction in life, we can often 'freeze' – not literally, of course, but through staying at home, not doing much, waiting for a great moment of insight to arrive. This is supported, of course, by ideas we have about what we should do when seeking direction. We know that Jesus went off into the wilderness for inspiration. On a different scale, when Oscar-winning film director Anthony Minghella had a life decision dilemma, he took himself off to a retreat. There is a powerful idea that removing ourselves to somewhere quiet and cut off from everyday life will offer inspiration. And for some people this certainly works. But these periods of respite may well be about putting to rest a previous cycle of our lives – giving it a resolution and conclusion – and then giving us the energy and space to start something new.

Sadie and her family moved out of London a couple of years ago:

> *I've always viewed myself as a flexible person, and was much more concerned about the children settling than I was about how I would adapt. I spent the first year or so feeling very unsettled – my life revolved around my diary and when I had my next meeting in London planned. Toward the end of this time I realised that I wasn't really putting any roots down in Dorset at all. My image of myself as a go-getting city slicker was much dearer to me than I'd ever realised. So I went to London for two days – and saw all my dearest friends, urging those who hadn't visited to come and see me down there. I told them all I wouldn't be back in London for at least three months. These two days had an almost ritualistic quality for me. I knew I was saying goodbye to the old me, and when I got back to Dorset I was ready to throw myself into life and work possibilities down there.*

While quiet meditation may help greatly if you are feeling directionless, you may find that you are inspired more quickly by action.

You will lose yourself in your calling

When we are doing something that we enjoy hugely and find deeply fulfilling, our brain produces more alpha waves. These are the brainwaves that are associated with creativity and they also make us feel relaxed but alert. We go into the state known as 'flow'. Again, if you feel directionless a bit of self-analysis can help.

Charting your flow exercises

What do you do in life that you find completely engaging – where time flies, you forget about any worries you have and you feel utterly satisfied at the end of it? For example, let's say you answer 'shopping'? Well, you could set yourself up as a professional shopper or an image consultant, or ask yourself what this pleasure in shopping is about. In my case, the explanation would be that I find looking at lovely things and making decisions about them very enjoyable. So in my day-to-day life, I arm myself with the best selection of mail order catalogues and, when I feel I need a boost, I have a peruse. Sometimes I buy; sometimes I don't.

If people are lucky, they manage to get similar satisfaction from what they do at work, as they do in their leisure time. My friend Brian gets great joy and a sense of satisfaction from sailing his boat as a hobby, 'making it run smoothly'. At work, he runs a retail company and again gets maximum satisfaction from 'making it run smoothly'.

So really be honest about what you find totally absorbing and keep asking yourself why. Then ask yourself: 'To get more of this in my life, can I look for more opportunities to do this in my existing working life? Or do I need to change direction completely?'

Your calling could have many contexts

Let's say your calling could be 'to teach'. You can do this at many levels: kids of all ages, further education or at university level. Or you could work in training in the private or public sector. You could write books or articles that help to teach people.

You could work freelance as a teacher like Henry:

> *I worked as teacher for twenty years and was a head master for the last five. There were increasing amounts of administration and I had always felt that my main purpose and strength was to be a good teacher – and that I could help other teachers to become highly effective. I retired early and now teach computer skills to individuals. I work a three-day week, my diary is full and I'm earning the same amount of money as a trainer. The work is highly satisfying and I get a great deal of appreciation from my students.*

While Henry's move may be to the detriment of our society, he has gained enormously personally.

Your calling won't respond to pressure

You can't make your calling speak to you. If you feel that you really haven't got an idea in your head about which direction you should take, and no matter how much you meditate or ask others for guidance nothing emerges, then you need to go on a concerted campaign. Find some recommended careers analysis counsellors (see page 227). Get some psychological profiling if you think you would find it useful. Put yourself out there and establish some new interests and challenges, or move to new surroundings. Learning new skills, challenging yourself and travel may be all part of this.

Your calling may be where you're at already

We love the myth of transformation. The Ugly Duckling and Cinderella contain the marvellous idea that complete reinvention can be possible. Because of the potency of this myth, it's tempting to start to think that if you change direction your life will need to be completely different. Most change isn't really like that. It's much more incremental, however much the sellers of plastic surgery would have us think differently. You may already be getting a great deal of satisfaction and a sense of fulfilling your purpose from where you are currently working, or perhaps just some small alterations to your role would bring your job and your purpose more in line.

Your calling changes over time

We change over our lifetimes and our purposes will change, too. While my purpose is definitely to teach, I would never have acknowledged that in, say, the 1980s. At that time, I saw my purpose as being a highly innovative and exciting consultant. Teaching would have been much too turgid an aim to admit to – even though that was what I was doing.

Spirit at work

As mentioned in Chapter One, a most frequently quoted authority on motivation is Abraham Maslow. First published in 1954, Maslow was a psychologist who came up with a 'hierarchy of needs', starting at the bottom with physiological needs (such as food and drink), then on to safety needs (security), up to love needs (sex and affection), followed by esteem needs (respect and the good opinions of others) and topped off by what Maslow called 'self-actualising' needs. His theory was that our motivational needs depended on the lower ones being met before we could proceed towards the 'higher order' needs, of which the ultimate was 'self-actualisation'.

Maslow described self-actualising people as being 'inner-directed', spontaneous, creative and child-like:

> *For instance, one woman, uneducated, poor, a full-time housewife and mother, did none of these conventionally creative things and yet was a marvellous cook, mother, wife and homemaker. With little money, her home was somehow always beautiful. She was a perfect hostess. Her meals were banquets. Her taste in linens, silver glass, crockery and furniture was impeccable. She was in all these areas original, novel, ingenious, unexpected, inventive. I just had to call her creative.*

While to our modern standards of emancipation, Maslow's description may sound rather patronising, it is a vivid description of how a self-actualising person lives.

I feel that I have something inside me called a spirit. It is the source of my enthusiasms, initiative and direction. It feels like it springs into action when I'm writing really well, or communicating really powerfully with people in workshops, or in coaching sessions. It is active when I'm having huge fun with my family and friends. It can't be measured – because it is unique to me – but that doesn't mean it doesn't exist.

So how do we engage our spirits at work? Well, if you're working for someone, then it helps to ensure that your values align to some extent with those of your employer. And it's really helpful to know before you take the job how your employer defines its purpose. It's the difference between feeling comfortable being as helpful as you can to customers because you know the purpose of your role is supreme customer service, and stalling your customers with petty company regulations, because you believe they must be enforced. And if you are clear about the purpose of your role and believe it to be one that suits your spirit, then appraisal of your effectiveness will be based on the extent to which you've achieved your role, rather than your performance on a range of tasks. When you are appraised on a range of tasks you are far less likely to be able to choose what you do to make your role effective and achieve your purpose. Your spirit will not be engaged to the same extent.

At the time of writing, Britain's once-successful Marks and Spencer retail chain is failing to achieve a recovery from several years of declining sales. No doubt much cost-cutting has gone on, as well as rationalisation of the business in order to make it more profitable. But something greater and less measurable is missing at Marks and Spencer, and it's to do with chemistry between the customers and the business. The spirit of Marks and Spencer is no longer evident – that pride of professionalism, good value for money and superb customer care that kept Middle Britain so loyal has wilted. And, of course, if the spirit of the staff in the business is strong and engaged, then customer loyalty will be, too. Businesses need to appreciate that staff morale and spirit is transferred in massive dollops to the suppliers and the public with whom they are dealing.

A little more prosaically . . .

While a calling may motivate us to learn skills, in order to fulfil ourselves we need to factor in realism, too. You are more likely to succeed in your dreams if they suit what you are good at. One way of analysing this is to look your skills in categories: people skills, information and data skills, physical skills, and creative skills, for instance.

You would be wise to show this description to someone

whose opinion you value, and to ask them whether there is anything missing there, or anything they think you should delete. If you are preparing a thorough description of yourself, it would be sensible to supply as many specific examples of these skills as you can.

Think about the highlights in your life's history and what they represented. These are good indicators of your most fulfilling values. You could ask yourself:

Did I demonstrate *competence* and *expertise?*
Did I *manage* things well, showing *political sense* and *people skills?*
Did I make things more *stable* and *secure?*
Did I exercise my *independence* and *self-sufficiency?*
Did I *create* something *new* here, which helped me to express who I am?
Did I manage to *balance* family and work better ?
Did I fulfil some *idealism* to make the world a better place?
Did I *overcome* some considerable *challenge?*

You may want to mull over these values for a while, to consider which are most important to you. Clearly, when an opportunity or role in an organisation matches your top values, then you are more likely to fulfil your calling. Ask yourself what this organisation regards as its purpose, and what the purpose of your role would be. This can help to clarify the values behind the organisation or the role you plan to take.

Finally, when you've identified your calling, you may want to work out pragmatically what resources you have to help you achieve it. Who do you know and what do you know? Can you let the influential know more about your aims? And ask them for help?

Thinking about values can often help us identify what is dissatisfying about specific parts of our lives. This may result in a decision to leave a relationship or a job, and to strike out on your own. And that's what the next chapter is all about.

7 Going Solo

'Hell is Other People.'
Jean-Paul Sartre

Have you noticed how tabloid newspapers love to carry stories of some celeb or other's infidelity, followed by flowery descriptions of their subsequent romance or romances? Time and time again we hear tales of people who've clearly been unhappy in relationships and have stayed in them until some better alternative has come along. And that's what the great majority of us do – hang on in there until we find someone else, while it may not be the most sensible thing to do. Wouldn't it be better to have a clean break, survive by ourselves for a while and then find someone new? To be able to live happily with ourselves, before trying to live happily with someone else?

But I suspect that it's the dread that we may never find someone that paralyses most of us into staying put. Better to be in a relationship that's going nowhere, than having no relationship at all. Now, psychologically this complicates things. We start the new relationship with unresolved feelings about our previous partnership, which is likely to make our feelings about our new relationship much more extreme. I expect some of you have experienced this: mild discontent for the first partner becomes hatred and guilt which turns the attraction for the new partner into a grand passion. In the throes of this terrible conflict it can be very difficult to keep a sense of reality about what is going on.

And something similar can happen at work. It's more comfortable to stay put in a job that we don't really find fulfilling, than risk the fear and insecurity that goes with looking elsewhere for greater satisfaction.

In this chapter I want to champion the idea that being content alone – calling on your own inner resources – is at the core of motivation. Many of us live lives where we give very little time and attention to our inner resources – we charge around being madly busy for our employers, family and friends – indeed, 'busyitis' is a status symbol, and admitting to having time on your hands and not a lot to do is an admission of failure. Nobody wants you because nobody is putting demands on you. In this chapter I want to investigate solo power: in personal relationships and professionally. We'll look at ending relationships (meaning friends and family, as well as lovers), and becoming self-employed with a portfolio career.

Being a writer, I would champion solitude, wouldn't I? My job involves spending a lot of time by myself, and solitude is probably the reason why a lot of writers suffer from depression. I'm lucky enough to balance this with a good social life with my family and friends, as well with workshops based on my books. It's fairly clear that we live in times where loneliness is epidemic, so you may be wondering if the last thing we need is more solitude. Well, loneliness and solitude are two very different things: we choose the latter but not the former.

A dance of dependency

Human beings are social creatures and we need one another to thrive – to create families, organisations, laughter, sport, schools and shops. These days more and more of us are living by ourselves – half of all marriages end in divorce and there are far more elderly people living by themselves. A lot of us may find ourselves more isolated than we wish – we may have to make more conscious efforts to connect to others through joining clubs, or evening classes or causes. We may live in sprawling urban developments that have no heart – the only focal points for inhabitants being a massive hyper-market. Many of us may feel a sense of detachment, alienation and meaninglessness about our everyday exist-ences. These feelings may increase as more of us work from home and engage more with technology than face-to-face with others.

So why on earth am I banging on about the need to happily handle solitude, when loneliness and a sense of isolation seem to be so prevalent? Well, because one is entirely dependent on the other. We are constantly nego-tiating our need for connection with others with our need for individuality and separateness. Without others we would go mad – other people give us reality checks on what we are thinking and feeling. However, when we over-connect with others, we may feel that our own identity is insecure and that we are entirely constructed by the reactions and responses of others.

Katherine, a civil servant, tells her story:

There have been times in my life where I have been very lonely. When I had my first child, for instance, I knew that I was changing a busy, very people-oriented working life a very different routine. A friend who had gone through a similar change advised me to get out everyday and to go to places where there were people – shopping centres, cafés and parks. It was great advice. I've never drunk quite so much cappuccino, but I met other mums and witnessing outside life going on kept me sane. A few years

*later when I was expecting my second child, my husband,
who is a diplomat, got posted to Switzerland. This was much
harder because there was so much readjusting needed for all
of us. I just made one dear friend who had two small children
herself and she was a godsend and a lifeline. Though I
regard myself as a fairly self-possessed individual, these
experiences made me realise just how important other
people are.*

Ultimately, we are responsible for ourselves.

What loneliness feels like

In my previous book, *Irresistibility*, I described the differences between introverts and extroverts. The more extrovert a person, the more important the stimulation they get from others will be. The more introvert a person, the more important the contact they get from external reality through others will be. When extrovert people get lonely, then, they will feel bored and empty because of a lack of stimulation from other people. When introvert people get lonely, they will feel out of touch with reality, because of a lack of contact with others.

But many of you reading this will have experienced very pleasurable times alone. Sometimes I love nothing more on a Friday evening than to shut the door on the rest of the family and to cook a slow simmering stew or an almond and orange cake. The activity is all-consuming and I am entirely absorbed in it – other people would just be an unwelcome distraction. Yet I love it when they tuck in later and admire my culinary worth . . .

Relationship failure

As tragic figures like Princess Diana illustrate, it's possible to live in a charade of a relationship and still feel desperately lonely. Relationships often fail because we don't understand how differently our partners interpret things. Despite the sky-high sales of books like *Men Are from Mars and Women Are from Venus*, we still assume that we can make other people become what we want them to. We believe that because we have a few glaringly obvious things in common, our goals will be common, and that we can really understand another person and work out what exactly makes them tick. These assumptions prevent us from trying to get anywhere near understanding how other people view things and what interpretations they are making of events. We get caught up in cycles of blame and recrimination that take us nowhere.

Getting out

When you're in a relationship that is making you feel lonely and unhappy, or a friendship or business relationship that is no longer working and you don't know what to do, there are some helpful questions you can ask:

- Are you able to sit down and discuss the different assumptions that you and the other person are using about your relationship and its goals?
- Is the relationship too important to you in your life? For instance, would a demanding business relationship be tolerable if you had more outside interests and a more involving personal life?
- What are the trade-offs in the relationship? In other words, what do you give them and what do they

give you? In what might be described as a 'traditional relationship', where he works and she stays at home, he gives courage and she gives confidence, she gets money and he gets security, she gives affection and he gives status, he gets financial responsibility and she gets parental responsibility. Have you compromised too much or too little over these?

- Can you get what's missing from the relationship elsewhere, if the core of it is sound? Sex, intimacy, excitement, glamour, attention, kindness can all be got elsewhere if you've the imagination.

Breaking it

There's nothing for it. You've decided you want out. So the first thing to do, bearing in mind this dance of connectedness and individuation in which we are all engaged, is to find yourself a supporter – a good friend or two who will see you through this. And I think very often that friends are more helpful than family in these circumstances; they are freer of family patterns of influence that may be unconsciously at work. Warn them that you may be calling on them fairly frequently over the next few months and would be happy to do a return match whenever needed.

The next thing to do, if at all practical, is to distance yourself physically from the person. Take a holiday, rent a property on the other side of town, go and stay with your Aunt Maisie in Eastbourne for a couple of weeks. Get yourself out of the other person's sphere of influence as much as possible and take a symbolic trip.

Distract yourself. Throw yourself into work, socialising

(but not with a view to meeting someone new), or go through a 'mad for fashion and make-up' phase. Master Thai cooking and get a cat or a dog. But remember: they're for life, unlike your last relationship.

Resolve to stay solo for the time being.

Make a list of all the things you can now do, which your last relationship prevented you from doing. This may include items like: cutting your toenails where and when you like, squeezing the toothpaste from the middle of the tube, filling the dishwasher in the haphazard fashion that you favour, or having Heinz Cream of Tomato Soup for four subsequent suppers. Celebrate this new freedom.

If you find yourself obsessing about your ex-partner, allocate an hour a day to 'fretting time'. Do nothing in this hour apart from worrying and thinking about the other person. Then, the rest of the time, forget them. This is greatly beneficial, because while allowing you to vent your feelings, it also encourages you to get on with your life.

Solo joy

Even though you may have instigated the end of your relationship, it's very likely that you will feel a sense of loss. Going through any change, we often underestimate the need to deal with feelings of loss – whether they are related to a job, social circle, home or lover. We try to cure the pain we are feeling by rushing into some new entanglement.

Better instead to allow ourselves a period of recovery, where we are particularly solicitous about our health and well-being, the people with whom we choose to spend our time, and what we spend our time doing. Taking up new interests can be helpful, too – provided they are not too demanding.

Sandi is an account manager in advertising:

> *Just after my divorce I really wanted something to occupy my mind so I started a part-time degree at my local university. I didn't really feel very confident about it and it wasn't until I had attended several study group meetings that I realised how the divorce had affected me. My self-esteem was really very low and when people complimented me on my work or appearance, or laughed at comments I made in the group, I was shocked. They were responding to me in a way I didn't expect, and I realised I had come to think of myself as a complete failure, rather than being more philosophical about the relationship not working. It was just great to be in an environment where people responded to you just on what you brought to the party.*

You may need to embark on an informal programme of building your self-possession. It may feel strange going for walks by yourself, or even to see a film. But, hey, what the heck; you are going through a necessary period of 'me-itis' here. You might want to embark on some sort of personal development programme or course, where you will be encouraged to talk about yourself a lot and to find yourself interesting. If you've been downtrodden in the relationship and need to relearn to stand up for yourself, then some assertiveness learning will help. Your local adult education college may well provide this.

Learn to enjoy the quiet contentment of solitude

It's useful to try and identify what your instant response is when confronted with a challenge. Some of us immediately try to buy something – a book or a counselling session

– others will immediately phone up friends or relations. Still more of us will hit the Gordon's.

But there is another alternative: use solitude and thought to make decisions and to get clarity. Try to get in touch with what your intuition is telling you and then seek the opinions and help of others. Remember that you have within you the best self-knowledge: it's only *your* self-knowledge that's been with you through the thick and thin of your life so far. Tap into that pool. Some people find it helpful to jot down dreams as soon as they wake to achieve some symbolic guidance.

Leaving the organisation

It's estimated that it takes most of us two to three years to realise the dream of going self-employed, once we've had the idea. Many of us dream of working for ourselves; in actuality, it suits some personalities far more than others.

Are you ready to work solo?

Choose between the following words:

power. . . . . influence
push . . . . pull
control . . . . freedom
familiarity . . . . intensity
routine . . . . projects
teamwork . . . . self-determining
belonging . . . . independence
reliable . . . . responsive
managerial . . . . entrepreneurial
security. . . . . excitement

If a lot of your preferred words are in the left column, you will want to think twice about becoming self-employed. If the majority of your choices are in the right column, congratulations, you are showing strong inclinations to be a self-starting solo player.

But just before we discuss how to do this thing, we should consider a bleak list:

- You may worry about the mortgage
- You will become lonely
- You will wake up some days without a clue what to do
- Your idea may not work
- Your idea may be mad
- Your life will be extremely unpredictable
- You may have to change your view of yourself radically
- Your partner won't like it
- You may have to exert more self-discipline than you ever believed possible
- People at work will envy your courage . . . or gloat at your foolhardiness

If, despite all this, you are determined to pursue your vision of working for yourself, then . . .

Welcome to the wonderful world of working solo

In recent years the realisation has dawned on me that having a good quality of life is not about big earth-shattering matters; rather, it's all about the small things that we encounter on a day-to-day basis. The walk you share with the kids to school, the nourishing home-made soup you make at weekends, the weekly cappuccino or glass of wine with a good friend all make life immeasurably better. And these small things are vitally important in the solo working world.

Some of you are going to hate me now, but on a typical working day this is how my diary runs:

8.30am	get kids off to school
9.00am	gym and a swim
10.00am	into the office for e-mailing, phoning, planning and writing
1.00pm	lunch
1.30pm	meditation
1.50pm	back to work
4.00pm	see kids briefly
5.00pm	get tea ready and finish work

Now not all days are like this. Sometimes I stay overnight in different parts of the country to do workshops, or have very early starts and late finishes for the same cause. But I consider my usual routine to be fairly idyllic – especially as the room I work from has a balcony facing trees and the sea. Yes, I'm lucky; but I've made lots of trade-offs in moving out of London and cutting down my consultancy and training business. I earn less money, know fewer people who do similar work, sometimes feel strangely on the periphery of everything that's going on, and am viewed by some clients as weirdly provincial and therefore unsuitable. Well, that's just their loss, I say.

Making the transition

For some people, the move from conventional work to self-employment is a very easy one. They may find that in mentioning their plans to existing clients or customers,

work starts to stack up. Or, on announcing their intentions, in these days of companies contracting-out, they
may find that their employers still want to make use of their
services in a part-time, short-term contract capacity.

But for others, a considerable amount of reinvention
may be required and the most important step is to start
seeing yourself as . . .

You, the Business

Good and useful businesses solve problems for people. So
what problem will you solve? Once that's identified, you
need to work out whose problem you are solving and
how these people will get to know about you. Your means
of solving this problem should be something you feel
passionate about, and something you'd still want to do if
you won the lottery. You have to care greatly about the
purpose of your work in order to keep going through the
uncertainty, rejection and experimentation that undoubtedly lies ahead.

When people start to work for themselves they usually
have to be more flexible than they may have needed to
be in full-time employment. So rather than doggedly
pursuing the one thing that you do well, you have to be
prepared to take on challenges that may be new, rather
scary and tangential to what you regard as your main skills.
I am categorically not saying that you should sell yourself
as someone who can do everything – a mistake a lot of
people make when they first start out being self-employed,
because they are so worried about not finding enough
work – but that you keep an open mind about the forms
your expertise can move into. So, while my core activities
are running workshops and writing books, I've also had

opportunities to write and present a TV series, produce and write videos and tapes, and write and present for radio. We're talking portfolio working here.

Your portfolio insurance

Portfolio workers do different things for different people. It's not the same as being a self-employed freelance, where you may just work for long periods of time for one client. Instead, it's juggling at least two or three different projects – the way many women have run their lives for years – with domestic responsibilities, child-rearing and handling work simultaneously. Traditionally, men have had much more of a 'this is my one job and this is how I do it' way of defining themselves. Hardly surprising, then, that they find significant lifestyle changes like retirement and redundancy much harder to cope with.

Now, as we all know, very few jobs are secure and certain these days. When you go portfolio, you go into the heart of this uncertainty and grab it by the goolies. You are setting yourself up with a range of options. If the market dips in one area, so be it; you still have others remaining. It's not about being controlling and managerial, it's about negotiating your way around varying demands on your time and attention. Those who hold strong beliefs that life can be controlled, managed and made predictable are best avoiding the portfolio lifestyle.

Intimate niches

Marketing people are often heard to declare these days that 'marketing is now all about niche'. What that means is finding a group of customers who particularly want your products or services, 'narrowcasting' them so that you build up as much specific knowledge about them as you possibly can, and then selling them different things to meet their specific needs. Better to have a small, selective group of customers who you know well and can cater for infinitely, than blanket marketing a large and diverse group, on whom you can never quite get a handle.

This idea fits very well with the change people need to make when they move from large organisation employment to working for themselves. Working for a large organisation tends to be about large-scale activity and using that size to push people into doing what you want them do; economies of scale are often a useful bargaining point. Working for yourself is much more about intimate contact with your clients and customers, emphasising trust and the mutual knowledge you have about one another. It's about attracting people towards your skills and expertise, with them knowing you are a useful reliable resource who is enjoyable to do business with. This change is not always easy to make. Here's Rachel's tale:

> Before having children I was a sales director with one of the big building societies. After six years at home, I was ready to go back to work, but I really wanted to be my own boss. I retrained as careers advisor and thought I'd try and sell programmes into businesses aimed at helping people take care of their own career development within the organisation. As sales director, my approach had been extremely energetic and forceful, pushing the team constantly. A couple of salutary experiences where I had doors shut very firmly in my face made me realise I had to take a far more circuitous route in my new incarnation. I threw myself into networking and just letting people know what I did, set

> up a couple of open events that gave tasters of workshops,
> and gave a lot of free careers advice to potential clients,
> informally! This all took a lot longer than I'd planned but
> now I've a really strong practice which I run as and when
> I wish.

The web makes intimacy, useful one-to-one contact in business much easier. It is also a really effective means of reaching niche markets for whatever it is you are selling.

Reputation, reputation, reputation

In workshops people sometimes ask me to talk about 'reputation management'. This always bewilders me — the idea that something as vague and abstract as 'reputation' can be managed. We can, of course, be highly aware of how others perceive us. In truth, it's probably wise to be this way. But as for the idea of 'managing' their perceptions, well, I expect a number of high-flying politicians would have something to say about that . . .

But in what's been called the 'attention economy', the way you get yourself noticed matters greatly. Here are some pointers:

Be very good at what you do. There is no substitute for this. If you suspect you could improve, then get better. And because the environment is always changing, there is increasing scope for self-improvement. Having said that, however, there are definite periods in life where we have more energy and commitment available to bring to learning.

Act professionally. Be on time, look the part, and respond to your clients and customers as rapidly as you are able. Behave with integrity and directness.

Don't bother competing with others. In big company life, a huge amount of energy goes into seeing off the competition; in the much more personal solo market, there is no point expending energy like this. Distinguish yourself through what you value and care about, and just use other people working in a similar field as useful reflectors of what you should charge, standards to which you should and shouldn't aspire, and possibly as pals and advisors.

Remember the dance of dependency. OK, so you're out working solo, doing your own thing, but are you connecting enough to other people with similar interests. Do you have interesting ideas you can give to others at workshops, in trade-related publications, on your website?

Know what your customers value. People value consideration and kindness, accessible knowledge, uniqueness, a credible and consistent track record and pleasant behaviour. All these attributes help to build reputation.

Never, ever appear desperate. Enthusiastic, yes, but desperation is the biggest turn-off. You want to think long-term, aiming for quality work, rather than quantity.

Ask people to recommend you, based on their appraisal of your work. A parting shot of 'If you've appreciated (your service or product) then you'd do me a great favour by telling others' may be the most potent reputation-building device ever.

Portfolios in practice

Here are some concerns people have expressed to me about being portfolio people:

How do I get work to begin with?

Test your idea out on a few people, especially those with knowledge of your sector. If you're producing some written material or a website, continually ask them for feedback. Ask them, too, for suggestions about where you might look for business. Let people know what you are doing via chatrooms on the web. Research, research, research, through newspapers, trade papers, and the web, and by going to meetings and conferences. Find other portfolio people in related fields. If you are clear about the need you are meeting, then getting attention won't be difficult. Approach journalists in your specialist sector with ideas for stories featuring your new role. Realistically, you should be prepared for a drop in income. My story is fairly typical in that it took me about two years of self-employment to be earning a decent living. During that early period I subsidised my business through part-time teaching a couple of days a week.

How do I manage my time?

Experienced portfolio workers become programmed into repeatedly asking themselves 'Is this the best use of my time?' I don't want you to become sceptical, but some large companies employ people who don't ask this question. They fill their time setting up meetings with portfolio people in whom they only have a mild interest. Or rather more craftily they will get in a portfolio person with a particular area of expertise to pick their brains, get free advice and then use this advice themselves and never get in touch with that portfolio person again. Yes, you hear the strains of bitter experience here . . .

So check the purpose of meetings and how much a prospective client or customer knows about you beforehand. If it's an early-stage inquiry, then an e-mail, fax or letter may be a better way of dealing with it. The golden rule in consultancy is to share *what* you would do for clients but not *how*. Though you may feel desperate for work, learn to say 'no'. Yes, take challenges, but when you know something is really out of your area of expertise and not anything you wish to be known for doing well, say 'no' – but you know a friend who does . . .

Give yourself a break from constantly thinking 'Is this the best use of my time?' Have regular breaks of 'soft time' where you play with kids, study something in a rather open-ended way, play the piano, go for walks, and take off your watch to forget about time and concentrate on engagement. Really good for that brain, I promise.

How do I cope with the isolation?

'E-mail friends' who are also portfolio workers are a great support. Some people probably won't take your portfolio working very seriously if you work from home, so try to have a sacred area from where you work. I find it helpful to have relatively set hours, though, having said that, I love nothing better than doing overtime on a Saturday night and then bunking off on a Monday afternoon. With small children, set hours are helpful – obviously from the childcare point of view, but also because they quickly get into the habit of seeing you at certain times.

Successful portfolio people usually have 'being their own boss' as a slightly higher priority than 'the company of others'. So in psychological terms, we could describe this as self-determination taking priority over social contact. However, to avoid losing contact with the reality that is your market, staying in touch with others in similar fields, networking in your sector and just getting out and about in your field will help you to prosper and keep you sane.

At the beginning of this chapter I mentioned that we are all engaged in a dance of dependency with others throughout our lives, based on our connecting with one another and establishing our individuality. This chapter has been very much concerned with individuality. In the second part of this book we'll move on to how we connect with others and motivate them.

Part 2

Motivating Everyone Else

8 *Sugar and Slugs*

An English teacher was explaining the concepts of gender. 'Should the word "computer" be masculine or feminine?' she ventured.

Her male students suggested 'computer' should be feminine because:

* No one but its creator understands its internal logic
* The native language it uses to communicate with others is incomprehensible to everyone else
* Even the smallest mistake committed is stored in its memory . . .

Her female students suggested 'computer' should be masculine because:

* It needs attention to turn it on
* It contains loads of data but is still clueless
* It is supposed to help you solve your problems but half the time it *is* the problem
* As soon as you commit to one you realise that if you had waited a little longer you could have had a better model . . .*

This chapter looks at three highly significant differences between woman and men which affect motivation: emotional differences, communication differences and differences of purpose.

* Thanks to Debbie Griffiths' e-gag collection.

Denying the difference

During the writing of this book, I took part in a radio debate about masculinity and the extent to which it was under threat. One of the other speakers, a sociologist, took issue with me when I described some of the general differences between female and male brains. 'Biology is only a tiny part of it all,' he said, 'and it's not very significant.' This comment, I thought, could only come from a being whose biology excluded him from experiencing the hormonal storms and calms of periods, pregnancy and the menopause. If you've never experienced these, it must be fairly easy to believe that biology is of little significance.

It was politically correct for a while in the 1970s to pretend that women and men were the same. This is not, of course, the same as thinking that women and men should have similar degrees of opportunity. Denying there is a difference between people is as discriminating and identity-denying as more obvious forms of discrimination. And it puts pressure on the less powerful to try to perform as well in the more powerful group's environment and to use *their* criteria for success. That thinking has past now – thank goodness – and most of us are happy to acknowledge that girls will be girls and boys will be boys.

A motivating force

Biological differences between women and men are likely to create differences in what motivates us. In my view, it's vitally important that we understand these differences. We can understand our own motivation a bit better and also why the expectations of the opposite sex may leave us feeling demotivated. We can also understand how better to motivate the opposite sex.

Karen works for a multinational telecom company:

> Before I became a mum, I had a high-flying job in telecommunications. It was a very dynamic, aggressive environment and very exciting to work there, as the business was increasingly successful. But after having two babies with just a couple of years between them, my whole attitude changed. I couldn't see myself as a 'corporate warrior' anymore; quite a lot of the motivational messages we were given just sounded downright silly, and I wasn't prepared to put in hugely long hours. To begin with I thought it was me – maybe I'd 'gone soft' in motherhood – but when I was at work I was as focused and sharp there as I had ever been. Looking round the company I realised that the vast majority of executives were testosterone-throbbing young men in their late twenties and early thirties. The board was entirely male. My motivation now was very different from theirs – I wanted to progress and be fulfilled but in a more balanced, thoughtful role. I was lucky enough to move across to change roles into a much more research- and project-based role, with freedom in how I worked, and performance based purely on results.

A piece of research from the USA vividly demonstrates how sex differences can affect motivation. A large corporation was attacked for not promoting enough women, even though it had a vigorous affirmative action policy to redress discrimination. Research into this problem found that female clerks held very different attitudes to their male colleagues: they were far less willing to relocate, they did not want to work long hours, far fewer of them regarded their jobs as the first rung on the ladder and, ultimately, they viewed their work as something they did for money and for the social elements. Just under half of the women said they would like part-time jobs, while just a fifth of the men expressed a similar desire.

While research like this can be interpreted quite rightly to press the need for a more family-friendly workplace, it also reflects inherent basic differences between what women and men want.

Girls who like guns and boys who like babies

Now you might be reading this and inside feeling, 'No, no, that's not me at all.' What I'm talking about in this chapter are *generalised* differences between women and men. During foetal development, it's thought that there are three opportunities for the foetus to be more or less affected by testosterone, the masculinising hormone. Some of you out there, then, will have feminised brains in male bodies and some of you will have masculinised brains in female bodies. In which case, please be patience with these generalisations and remember that it's most useful to see masculinity and femininity as opposing ends of a continuum, with each of us as individuals fitting in at different points:

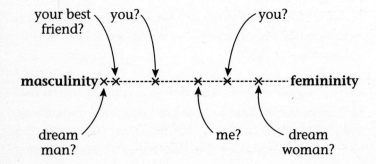

And then there's conditioning . . .

An Australian university has discovered that since the 1940s the apparent pitch of female voices has dropped a couple of tones. Have female vocal chords altered their biology? Has there been some evolutionary change making us sound a bit more blokey? Not a bit of it. It seems that as women have achieved greater equality, their need to speak in the fragile tinkley tones of a tragic old-film heroine – like Celia Johnson in *Brief Encounter*, or the Queen – has disappeared. Instead of sounding like we're on the verge of needing revival with smelling salts, we've gone all gravely and strong like Kathleen Turner.

This illustrates then how social conditioning and expectations affect our behaviour. Life is still harder for those among us who feel themselves to be very masculine women or very feminine men, and who want to express those inclinations through our personal presentation and how we live our lives.

And the baby business . . .

There is nothing like having kids to emphasise the differences between women and men. Many women and men discover capacities for love and patience that they never knew they had. Many women unexpectedly discover reserves of stamina and many men discover a strong sense of responsibility of which they were perhaps unaware. In many relationships, the man's career takes on extra importance post-babies. Despite some couples successfully sharing childcare, and some high-profile women, like top-earning businesswoman Nikki Beckett, leaving the kids at home with Dad, it is still a given in our society that the caring of children should be the woman's top priority.

And when we work, as the majority of us do, the organising of childcare tends to be our concern.

State of play

Before we go into the main sections I think it's useful to have a quick summary of the current state of play:

Clever girls, successful men

Girls are better at exams, but men are still paid more and there are more of them are at the top. There is only one female chief executive, Majorie Scardino, among the one hundred companies in Britain. Women make up half the workforce and, in increasing numbers, they are opting out of the 'boys' world of organisational life in order to start their own businesses.

Juggling women, work-defined men

Many women seem to feel they do two jobs – running the family and bringing up the kids – as well as their day jobs. Women report spending far more hours in domestic duty than do men; in fact, a recent study showed that women still do some 60 percent more housework than their male counterparts. For many men, a career is absolutely central to how they define themselves and their identity is very bound up with what they do. When they retire, then, or something prevents them working, like being made redundant or experiencing ill-health, they find this change more traumatic than women do.

Longer living women, freer living men

On average, women live longer than men, and are more likely to pay attention to health and medical matters. Men tend to abandon their families more readily than women, and go off and 'do their own thing'. And our image of 'man as hunter' perhaps makes us more tolerant of how men behave; it's hard to imagine President Hillary Clinton getting away with the serial infidelity her husband enjoyed.

Emotional differences

When women and men are shown the same pictures, they see different things. Women will tend to describe the people and feelings; men will tend to describe the objects and the action. And female and male eyes do actually see things differently: women having greater sensitivity to the longwave spectrum of light and greater sensitivity to red as a colour. Female babies are able to identify faces and expressions before boy babies, who gurgle as happily at a balloon as they do at a human being. Some adult male behaviour may question whether they have moved on from this: when my partner's been out for a few drinks with friends and comes in and gurgles at my apparently sleeping form, it makes me wonder . . .

Emotions in the brain

Men's brains are tidier places that those of women. Their emotions are neatly compartmentalised within one part of the brain, while the typical female brain has emotion-producing parts spread over the two lobes of the brain, with far more connection between those two lobes. Hence the two very differing interpretations of what is going on: the male brain − if it sees it at all − will see the emotional components as just one aspect of a situation; the female brain will be much more sensitive and holistic in the interpretation of the emotional components. And because the female brain produces a wide and sensitive perspective on emotion, women are more predisposed to read emotion and to guess the meaning behind it. When women and men are shown people portraying strong emotion on film, women consistently guess the cause of the emotion behind the expression with greater accuracy than men.

Greater connection between the emotional parts of the brain and the parts that handle verbal ability give women a greater capacity to talk about their feelings. On the other hand, men often express their emotions through actions, rather than words. Judith, a workshop participant, told me this story:

> I stayed at home bringing up the children for many years, then went back to work in my mid-forties for a while, part-time. I'm now fifty. Six months ago I applied for a full-time senior management role in my organisation, really just for the hell of it, as I didn't think I'd stand a chance of getting it. Well, surprise, surprise, I did . . . My husband said he was thrilled and very proud of me . . . but I thought he might have some feelings, too, that he wasn't expressing. Our home life would change quite dramatically with me out at work full-time in a demanding role. Just a week before I started my job he announced his attention of completely renovating our bathroom and toilet and that he was going to do this himself. Previously we had always employed others to work on our home, and there were no new circumstances that should cause this to change. It meant, of course, that I was starting my new role and going through those critical first weeks without a decent bathroom and loo at home and quite a lot of disruption. I don't think he meant it maliciously at all, or even consciously, I just think he felt

that his life was going to be disrupted by my career change and that he felt uncomfortable about it. He wasn't able to articulate this to me, so he instinctively went in and created some actual physical disruption first.

Action man

You are more likely to succeed in motivating a man if you suggest a course of action. Let's take the example of spending more time with the children. A mum – with her female brain – will quite enjoy sitting around pottering with the children, chatting to them and socialising. A father is far more likely to enjoy trips to the museum, football, swimming and movies, where the closeness and relationship is endorsed through doing and action. So moaning about him 'spending more time with kids' is likely to be far less effective than suggesting he *do* something with them.

Different responses to stress

Recent research by Professor Shelly Taylor at the University of California has demonstrated how female and male responses to stress are different biologically. The male response involves testosterone, which makes the man ready to fight or flee. The female response involves oxytocin, which produces loving feelings and creates what's been called a TAB response, standing for 'tend and befriend'. This explains why many of us under pressure like to pick up the phone and have a long chat with a friend. Under pressure, men are more likely to benefit from opportunities to burn off that aggression and women are more likely to benefit from opportunities to have lots of contact with good friends.

Independence and interdependence

Greater levels of testosterone make men more aggressive, single-minded and eager to pursue independence. Stronger drive means that men are more easily angered and frustrated if their progress is impeded. A more connected, less compartmentalised brain makes women more sensitive to the feelings of others – more all-encompassing in their interpretations and in pursuit of connection with others. Female biology – with its hormonal swings – makes women more emotionally volatile. Men kill themselves more frequently, women suffer more frequently from depression. Time to move on to a cheerier note, I think.

Motivational fix

So what does this mean in terms of motivating men and women? With men orientated towards action, independence and things, the best way to appeal to a man's feelings is to make him feel useful. It's not coincidental that a man's favourite part of his body is often referred to as his tool. With women orientated towards connection with others and feelings, the best way to appeal to a woman's feelings is to make her feel appreciated, even cherished. It's hardly necessary to state it, but the easiest way to alienate a man is to make him feel useless and the easiest way to alienate a woman is to be insensitive to her. When we are motivating members of the opposite sex, we need to remember that we may be most effective using needs that are not top priorities in our own psychology. John manages a factory of about three hundred people:

> *A few years ago I'd read lots of management material about equality and I decided I'd put some of it into practice by*

*handling the guys in a way that was closer to the way I
handled women. I'd noticed that women seemed to like it
when you appreciated something they'd done or something
about their personal presentation. I knew it was a bit
unusual, but I thought I'd comment on changes in the guys'
appearance or when their behaviour was especially
intelligent towards others. I'd completely overlooked that
when you do this other guys think a) you must be gay and
somewhat threatening because of this, or b) you've lost the
plot and are being inappropriately personal. Thinking again,
I realised that what the guys wanted to know and hear was
how effective they had been in solving a problem. If I
commented on their appearance in terms of their effectiveness in handling a difficult customer, and showing that we
took them seriously, it was OK. But just commenting on
presentation or behaviour itself – well we were getting a bit
nancy-boy here, weren't we?*

Communication differences

Never mind Mars and Venus. When you begin to look at
communication differences between men and women, it
strikes me as an absolute miracle that we manage to co-
exist fairly happily in the same galaxy.

Problem-solving and problem-sharing

You get home from the office. You've had a terrible day.
Your secretary has been off sick, a client has cancelled an
enormous order, and you have pressing deadlines on
several important projects. When you get home, before
you sink speechlessly into a bottle of Merlot, all you want

to do is talk. You feel upset and frustrated when your partner listens, and then suggests that you would feel a lot better about everything if you changed jobs. Are you more likely to be male or female?

You get home from work. Things have not gone well. You were presented with a great deal of resistance to a proposal you made in a meeting, to which you had anticipated a very favourable response. The train on which you were travelling was stuck in a tunnel for forty-five minutes. When you get home, before you flop out senselessly in front of the television, all you want is sympathy. You feel irritated and misunderstood when your partner listens, and then suggests that you need to develop some stress-control techniques to cope with these minor blips that life throws at us. Are you more likely to be male or female?

When women talk about their problems, what they are looking for is empathy. Their philosophy tends to be 'a problem shared is a problem halved', whereas the male view tends to be 'a problem shared is one to be solved'. Men are very keen on rushing in with practical solutions to unhappy feelings: after all, men define their effectiveness in terms of doing, action and solution.

When men talk about their problems – and, generally speaking, they are less likely to do this than women – what they are looking for is support and agreement. The worse thing they can be offered is unsolicited advice, especially in the area of feelings – which is not well charted territory for the majority of men. This will only deepen any feelings of inadequacy they are experiencing.

And when a woman has what may sound like a glib solution presented to her problem, then she will feel as though she hasn't been heard, that her feelings do not matter, and that she is not being appreciated. Meanwhile, the man feels that her shirty response to his advice is evidence that she doesn't regard him as the effective problem-solver he knows himself to be.

And when a man receives unsolicited – and what he considers to be belittling – advice, he will feel that he is not the warrior-fixer he knows himself to be. He will feel that he has misplaced trust in the listener, and that she doesn't care for him. Chances are, he won't do it again – much safer to stew silently behind the evening paper. Not surprisingly, the advice-giver feels that his anger at her suggestions just confirms his lack of understanding of his own emotions. A most unhelpful cycle.

Motivational fix

So men listening to women's problems could benefit from giving plenty of attention to showing they've heard the feelings: 'So you felt misheard there' or 'You felt fed up about that'. Yes, guys, you get to play counsellor here! Women listening to men's problems could benefit from steering the conversation in the direction of what *action* could be taken to solve this problem. Yes, girls, you get to play co-commander here!

Nags and insults

For roughly half its life, the female body goes through monthly cycles of change. This female familiarity with physical change may make us feel more comfortable with it, and also to believe that others, like men, may be more responsive to change than they actually are. Why, we may even expect that they are capable of changing their behaviour!

Factor in here, too, the fact that women tend to be

other-focused and men tend to be self-focused, and you have a recipe for disaster. She believes people can change, she thinks he is selfish, she focuses on this and him, and it's nag, mama, nag . . .

The male orientation towards self and independence means that when men are in groups, their position in the pecking order and their status are incredibly important. This often gives male communication a robust quality: joshing one another and insulting being all part of this. Even when men are playing or working together in teams, aggression and seeking precedence in the pecking order is regarded as appropriate behaviour. Handing out insults is all part of this status-seeking, and though it may not be meant seriously, there is a clear aim behind it.

When we consider that women on the receiving end of these insults are likely to be more other-focused, and therefore more sensitive to their reactions, we have another recipe for disaster. He boosts his status by insulting her; she is deeply hurt because she is sensitive to others and actively seeks closeness.

Motivational fix

Women have to accept that there is no point in nagging. Far better to offer a clear carrot of the 'This will involve action/status-seeking' variety, and if he fails to bite frequently enough at that, well, there's a lot more red mullet in the sea. When men are insulting, just remember that emotional intelligence is tightly compartmentalised inside their little heads, and sometimes it's just impossible for them to make a good connection.

Men need to be sensitive to insulting women. Just remember that they are probably not as hell-bent as you are on establishing their position. They probably just want a quiet life, involving silk sheets, aromatherapy oils and a good giggle. When women nag you, just be flattered at how flexible and self-improving they imagine you to be.

Private and public worlds

Watch little girls in the playground and you will see lots of one-to-one conversations and secret sharing going on. Watch little boys and you are likely to see loads of action, shouting (including an ongoing volume competition), not a great deal of listening, and lots of marching and attacking.

I'm currently studying for a PhD, which involves a group of peer students studying their own group dynamics. We have lots of tortuous group sessions, where the guys try and achieve dominance, and the women on the whole say little. The guys say and make most of the contributions. (I try and have the odd stab at all this, standing up for the sisterhood.) The women are often found describing what they don't like in the toilets in twos and threes. They are very reluctant to make explicit what they do or don't like in the group.

Men do not differentiate greatly between public and private communication: if you're independent and seeking to establish your position in the pecking order, then speaking out in groups like meetings is all part of this. Indeed, many men, whether consciously or not, regard meetings as battlegrounds for dominance.

Women tend to be far more comfortable with what they consider to be private communication: this may take the form of gossip, secret-sharing, and revealing knowledge about the rich, famous, great or good. Yes, you probably know that most *Hello!* and *People* readers are girlies. At work, many women would naturally be happier discussing issues in twos and threes rather than in larger meetings, which involves them playing for prominence and dominance.

Another difference linked to our private and public preferences is the extent to which we are direct or covert in our meanings. Men are far more likely to 'Tell it like it is', while women are less self-focused, and tend to conceal their meaning and make it more covert. Take Sally, for example. She doesn't want to go to Geneva on behalf of her boss, Tom. When he asks her, she says, 'Oh, do you think you could possibly delay the meeting?' Tom stresses its urgency. 'Well,' says Sally, 'shouldn't you ask Bill whether he'd like to go first?' 'Please, Sally,' says Tom, 'can you just give me a straight yes or no?'

Motivational fix

If men really want a good discussion with a woman, they're best off doing it in a small group rather than a large one. They may need to ask the woman to be as direct as possible about what she thinks, feels and needs.

At the moment, the male model of how things should be done still prevails in the workplace. Women who want to get themselves noticed and get to the top have to get comfortable playing for dominance in meetings. Do this by saying something early on, such as, 'I'm sorry to interrupt . . .', then carry on and do. Sit prominently, either at the end of a rectangular table or in the middle of one of the sides. Or, with a round table, sit opposite the chairperson or the most powerful person present. Take up plenty of space on the table with folders and papers, to make yourself look significant. Sisters, we still need to use every tactic we can.

New-agers and scientists

Now I don't mean that women tend to be a bunch of irrational crystal-dangling channelling goddesses, while men are a bunch of Einsteinian test-tube enthusiasts. It's more linked to general orientation in processing the world and, therefore, how we communicate.

Possibly because of greater linkages between parts of the brain, women tend to be more holistic in their orientation and to be as interested in what's behind communication as they are in what's on the surface. When women interpret things they often like to get as full a picture as possible with a fair amount of detail.

This female 'detailed miniature' way of seeing things may account for what's known as 'female intuition'. Intuition is a leap of connection between brain cells – often between what you are receiving from someone's behaviour with information brain cells that your unconscious memory are holding. So, for instance, you might meet a stranger for whom you feel an intuitively strong attraction, without consciously remembering that something about him is strongly reminiscent of your first lover. But that will be the connection that is being made.

Men tend to be far more orientated towards linear viewpoints, fact and information, to take communication at its surface value, and to pay attention to content as much as behaviour. When men interpret things, they often like to get as clear a picture as possible, to be analytical about it, and to theorise, abstract and see form.

The male 'bold abstract' way of seeing things may account for men being better at things like map-reading. This require spatial intelligence, but also the ability to glance at something and quickly extract a form or shape of direction from it. In my view, this ability is more than completely offset by men being unable to ask for directions because of a perceived loss of face when maps are missing or don't work . . .

We might expect, then, that these different ways of interpreting make for different ways of taking decisions. The female preference is to take in as much as possible before making the decision, while the male preference is for clear, linear logic. Guess who usually gets there first. but who later finds out there's more to it that he first thought?

Motivational fix

Where your aim is to motivate a man, you are most likely to be effective when you have a clear linear form to your content. Men like to hear the route through the forest, signposted from A to B to C, with a clear idea of what should be viewed at each of those signposts. Their concentration is focused on a narrow range of points, and they will ignore distractions.

Where your aim is to motivate a woman, you are most likely to be effective when you have a fairly detailed description of the setting and connections between ideas. Women like to hear some of the interesting trees featured in the forest, and where plants of similar type can be espied. Their attention likes to range over a subject in all its complexity.

Differences of purpose

Women and men, as we might expect, will often have different goals in terms of 'what makes a good woman', and 'the makings of the ideal man'.

Respected men, cherished women

With many men on a quest for independence, one of their pet aversions will be the feeling that they are being smothered and that there is insufficient distance between themselves and others.

With many women seeking connection, one of their pet aversions will be the feeling that they are being abandoned, left alone and that there is too much distance between themselves and others.

Motivational fix

To motivate men, you have to give them plenty of space. They have to feel that options are being presented to them, and that they have power of choice. The empathetic 'I know how you're feeling' approach may seem completely inappropriate to them. Also, too much emphasis on common ground may make them feel engulfed, and that their independence is being threatened. So let them know the parameters in which they can operate, the space available and your interest in what course of action they intend to take to achieve the goal. Remember, we are talking compartmentalised brains here!

To motivate women, remember that they appreciate support, encouragement and appreciation. If you want them to develop independence, ask them how great a degree of involvement they would like you to have. How often would they like to review progress, for instance? Let them know that you can be contacted, and are in the background in a supporting role. Otherwise, you risk them feeling a sense of panic over 'My goodness, I'm out here alone and on my tod!' We are talking connected brains here, remember!

Pacifist women, war-like men

Many women find it difficult to disagree and argue because they like personal approval, dislike conflict and sense that disagreeing makes them unattractive. How wrong they are if a survey of British male members of parliament is anything to go by. It found that Margaret Thatcher was regarded as being far more attractive than Denise van Outen – obviously some reflection of the sort of men who are attracted to politics. Whatever turns them on . . .

When we look at male behaviour in a sales team at work, or on the football or rugby pitch, the urge to fight on behalf of the group is a highly regarded one. Male bonding is all about using aggression collectively to fight the enemy – and an individual male lacking in aggression will suffer.

Motivational fix

When you want to keep a woman motivated, emphasising the development of relationships and the power of connection will help. Being aggressive towards her may scare her – unless she's Thatcheresque and rather admires others using her own tactics.

When you want to keep a man motivated, emphasising the challenges that lie ahead and the good battle that needs to be fought – yes, in my experience, words like strategy and tactics tend to be popular with men – will help you inspire more effectively. Don't back away from an argument, but enter into it with good humour. And don't take it too seriously – regard it as locker-room sparring.

A final word: Do I play the game or opt out?

For women who want to have it all, with a good relationship, children and a career, there seems to me to be three main options:

Go into mainstream organisational life which, with some exceptions (like parts of the BBC, cosmetic companies, some publishing businesses), tends still be heavily male-dominated at the top. Mimic the chaps through tactics like overpowering everyone else at meetings, and get better at these tactics than they are. But give yourself a healthy outlet for your inner girlie. Even Margaret Thatcher relished clothes, make-up, hair, Cecil Parkinson and Ayurveda, for example.

Secondly, try to change the definitions of conventional success. Lobby on behalf of women in the mainstream organisational life, mentor and network frantically, and make yourself into a role model for others. Exhausting this one, but admirable.

Finally, opt out and do your own thing. Start your own business, or practise whatever it is you want to do professionally on your own terms. Where you are self-sufficient, energetic and determined, this is probably one of the best ways of balancing your time and effort. For men who'd like it all, too: do your own thing, or join an organisation where there are lots of understanding women.

So there you go: women, men and the differences between them. It's a crucial part of understanding different approaches to motivation. It's time to tackle that daunting Medusa or scary Schwarzenegger. Now you know their secrets, they are yours for the motivating . . .

9 Come on Let's Work

'Work is love made visible.'
Kahlil Gilbran

When I talk to people about motivating ourselves at work, they often comment along the lines of: 'Motivating people? It's easy, isn't it? You just pay them more money'. And so employers, particularly in these times of low unemployment and a shortage of good workers, offer potential recruits performance-related pay schemes and all sorts of other financial carrots.

Money, money, money

While it is, of course, demotivating to be paid less than you think you are worth, when groups of workers take industrial action because they want more pay, it is rarely on the basis of pay alone that they protest. They protest because they are paid less *compared* to people in similar or complementary roles. So nurses, for instance, will take a position on the *fairness* of their earnings in relation to the wages of firefighters, ambulance drivers, police officers and doctors, perhaps. The amount of money they earn reflects the relative value society places on their contribution, influenced by market forces. And that may seem a very odd relative value, indeed, when you compare the wages of a top nurse with that of a top footballer. Still, when the cabinet's largely female, I'm sure that will change.

And if it is so easy to motivate people with money, why is it that so many of the well-off keep working? For the sake of enjoyment, perhaps, but also for what money represents to them: freedom, security or even a sense of superiority over others. Here's what Michael, a company director, said:

> In truth, I've probably had enough money to live off comfortably for a couple of years, since I floated my company on the stock market. But my assessment of my financial worth has always been viewed in security terms. So I've always asked myself whether I've enough through the perspective of disaster scenarios. It started off with what was enough in terms of me personally being completely incapacitated, then I added a complete crash of all the money markets, a collapse of the property market and my wife being completely incapacitated, too. It was only when I worked out that we would still survive financially, even if all that happened and the five members of my family required round-the-clock nursing due to complete incapacitation, that I started to think I had enough. You probably think I'm nuts, but making money has always symbolised getting security for my family. I don't think it's coincidental that my own family had a small business which failed when I was quite small. And although I remember very little about it, clearly the anxiety which was around played its part.

Money by itself is a neutral commodity: it's the longings and fantasies that we project on to it that gives it its value – and makes us want more of it.

Can't buy you love

When companies take the rather blinkered view that money alone will motivate their employees, they lay themselves open to problems. The first one is that they often overlook that performance is about what the person brings to the role plus *what is happening in the environment*. So you could be performing brilliantly in your role, but there could be all sorts of detrimental factors in the environment – such as recession, for instance – which means that you do not get the results for which you were aiming. To be useful and fair, any assessment of performance, then, needs to factor in those environmental influences.

When people are given the carrot of performance-related pay, it can make them selfish and over-concerned with looking good as individuals. It can be detrimental to team performance and the goals of the business. When businesses assume that their employees are entirely motivated by money, it weakens the psychological contract: the complex set of trade-offs between business and employee. Trade-offs like: 'You, the business, give me security; I give you commitment'. The assumption that people are entirely motivated by money gives rise to a short-termist approach.

Jim is a sales director in a call centre:

> I try to avoid hiring people who are just motivated by money. I know they won't last because someone else will come along, offer them more money, and they'll go. I want people here who will stick around a bit longer, and I try very hard to motivate them through a range of benefits.

And what about the effect on morale? Some of us like ourselves less when we are defined by others as being greedy and purely motivated by money. So that annual review we get, where we go through the ritual of discussing the 7% rise, may not be an entirely pleasant experience. I recently had experience of this, when I was waiting for news of a big project to be confirmed. If the project didn't happen, I was to get a sum of money for my preparation work. When the client was talking to me about how long the decision was taking, she said, 'Well don't worry, because you'll get £X in a couple of months anyway.' 'No,' I wanted to say, 'you're getting me wrong – it's the challenge and scale of the project that's motivating me. The money is just what the market pays for such a service.'

Thinking motivation

Think about a time when you were feeling really great at work. Was it purely about making money or were there other feelings attached, too? You will know from this answer what really motivates your performance.

So if you've not guessed it by now, in this chapter we look at things that motivate us at work – other than money – and they are:

- meaningfulness
- freedom of choice
- performance and progress

These are 'intrinsic' rewards – ones that make you feel good immediately rather than ones that you will experience once a year, like the annual bonus.

Lawrence is a retail store director:

> We work on a profit-share basis in our company, and once a year we all get a bonus based on how the business has done. While it is a great motivator, I don't think the once-yearly payment really matters that much. What matters is that everyday we all have a great sense of camaraderie and pulling together to make this business work well – and the atmosphere around here is usually tremendously warm and positive. Even when the bonus has been disappointing, the feeling of us 'all being in this together' has kept most of our spirits high.

Sound like a good motivational force? It can be, and I'll get on to that in a minute. What we need to consider first, however, is the idea of environment, and the problems associated with profound environmental change.

Old and new economies

People talk a lot about the 'new economy', and despite press reports that e-business is threatened and that the revolution is in jeopardy, there is no doubt that business has changed dramatically under the influence of IT, globalisation and the weakening of traditional institutionalised authority, such as the church, the law, governments and the American presidency.

The old economy favoured a 'command and control' type approach to motivating people at work: reward them for good behaviour – and, more frequently, punish them for bad – which really implied that people needed to be controlled in the way that we train puppies. Often this approach kept people at work slightly scared. If we use the idea that we can only move in three ways with each other: towards, away from, and against, we might guess that when people are treated rather like small puppies the direction they move in is away from the people doing the treating.

And what this approach to motivating people over-looked was that we are capable of setting goals as individuals (in fact, a lot of us are very keen on this), that we tend to monitor our own performances, to want to do better and succeed and to understand ourselves and change ourselves, which is learning.

There is a mindlessness in the command–and–control approach to motivating because people are rewarded purely on the basis of the behaviour they exhibit: there is no sense at all of people using their initiative, or an under-standing of the greater purpose being things that matter. Why should people then accept change when they are regarded as pure operatives, rather than people whose opinions count and who are capable of producing improvements?

In the new economy – with its necessary flexibility and, need for knowledge workers, and the breakdown of barriers between countries and people via communications – the challenge for businesses is to find new ways of getting a competitive edge. There is no doubt that finding and keeping committed people, who initiate and implement change of their own volition, is the best way of doing this. Where uncertainty is all around – with the people at the top of the organisation dealing with the biggest uncertainties – those a bit further down still need to have the confidence and understanding to deal with lots of the others.

And people who take initiatives will not remain motivated if they are treated like little puppies. They need to be recognised as fully formed self-determining adults who are capable of setting their own goals, altering their behaviour if feedback suggests it, monitoring their own performance and seeking to improve this performance in an ongoing way.

In the old economy, many people, especially in the traditionally 'secure' sectors like banking, expected their jobs to last for life and for the company to look after them. In the new economy, very few people expect that and, as a result, employees generally tend to feel less company loyalty. They are dispassionate about the rewards of employment, knowing that if they do not get what they want from a particular employer, they can probably easily and quickly go elsewhere. The companies who will be winners in this new economy will be the ones who succeed in motivating and thereby retaining their most talented staff – and, in doing so, making these very staff members take and implement important organisational decisions for themselves.

Meaningfulness

When left to our own devices, human beings will seek meaning for themselves. We will create structures – be they mud huts or book plans – and we will organise tasks, whether that involves collecting some straw or writing to several commissioning editors. And behind those structures and tasks, we will have a clear sense of purpose.

When asked what they do for a living, many people will reply by describing a series of activities; for instance, I would say I write books, run workshops and run a small business, with all that is involved in that. And if someone were measuring my performance from outside, they might suggest that I write more books, or run bigger or more frequent workshops, or expand my business considerably. But that would not suit my purpose: which is to make work psychology accessible and fun for people. And more importantly, perhaps, it would stop being fun for me!

My purpose makes me want to write interesting and creative books, to run workshops as special events that matter to everyone involved, rather than run-of-the-mill training courses, and I certainly don't want to end up managing an expanding training company (I did once before and it was horrible . . .). So it is a very definite purpose that shapes my choices.

With a definite purpose in mind, what we should and should not do in our jobs becomes much clearer.

Let's say you are working in a shoe shop. The rules of your business say that you should aim to serve as many customers as possible every hour. But the overridding purpose of your role – and the business, as you understand it – is to give absolutely outstanding customer care. A customer comes in and falls in love with a pair of shoes that you do not have in her size. If you are following the rules, you just tell her you're sorry and get on to the next customer. But if you are following your purpose, and the business's top purpose, you ring up another branch of your business, find out if they have the size in stock and, if they do, get those shoes biked round to your customer's home. You then have that customer's undying loyalty for life. Reader, I know this, because fifteen years ago I was that customer and that particular business is always my first port of call for any footwear needs. In this country, that level of customer service was extremely unusual and, as a result, highly memorable.

Research into successful organisations almost always shows that they share a common characteristic – an emphasis on values over and above profit. As consumers we will know John Lewis for honesty and integrity ('never knowingly undersold'), we will know Amazon.com for amazing customer service, and we will know the Virgin Brand for its emphasis on fun and novelty. These organisations carry greater meaning than simply turning a buck.

For us as individuals, there will be as many different definitions of meaningfulness as there will be different values. Some descriptions of meaningfulness I have heard include: 'making a difference', 'helping people live their lives more fully', 'creating beauty', 'making things more efficient', 'doing something significant in the world', 'giving others pleasure', 'using my creativity to make something useful for people', 'helping things to work well', and 'treating people to brilliant service and making them feel good'.

Job decisions

If you're considering a job offer, 'clarity of purpose' can be a helpful criteria for whether or not to accept. Where the job *purpose* is emphasised, you are likely to have more choice over what you do, and when and how you do it. Appraisal will be on the basis of the extent to which you are achieving this purpose. In contrast, when your job is described in terms of detailed task analysis, this is less likely to be so. You are far more likely to find yourself being appraised for tasks that you do not consider central to your effectiveness. This seems to me to be a very critical element of job choice: is the organisation one that is purpose-centred or task-centred, with the mindlessness that this may involve?

Where you are feeling dissatisfied in a job, then discussion and clarification about its purpose can be really helpful. You might even find that you can invent a new purpose or at least change roles where the purpose is much more suited to your values and liking.

Increasing meaningfulness

The meaningfulness of what we do is something that probably preoccupies us at certain times in our lives. When we are starting out in our career, then we are likely to be far more concerned with competence. And if we're not concerned with competence, or have some attention left over, then it's probably being diverted to really important concerns, such as getting one's leg over . . .

Meaningfulness and questioning the significance of what we do is likely to be of greater relevance when we are quite established at something. Indeed, it could be another way of describing the good old mid-life crisis. Tim's story is a good one:

> *I had been in advertising for about twenty years, when I started to get quite strong feelings that I wanted to change my life. I felt caught up in a horrible cycle of working manically, earning huge amounts and then spending them manically. At weekends I was completely and utterly exhausted, as was my partner. Then I got ill with a fairly serious digestive problem that required surgery. The doctor advised a change of lifestyle. So we moved a little way out of London, took the kids out of private education and into the local state school, and I got the agency to agree to me working a two-day week as a self-employed consultant.*

With my partner we decided we would set up a small consultancy offering advice to charities and interest groups on how they could advertise their causes more effectively. We would keep our fees under a certain ceiling that our client base could afford. We've been going for about three years now, work when we want to, earn less and spend less. We see far more of our kids because of working from home. Our roles are very clearly divided in the business and we have separate offices in the home – an insurance policy that seems to be paying off in terms of us not heading in the direction of the divorce courts, both working and sleeping together. Our London visitors – who thought we'd lost our marbles when we made the move – now seem quite envious of our situation . . .

Where you want to help others find their work more meaningful, you may find it useful to:

Ensure people work on whole tasks. What would you rather tell people you did? Looked after all the chief executive's day-to-day affairs, or made her coffee, kept her diary, ordered her cars, took her calls, and got her out of the office on time each evening? We get far more satisfaction from working on whole tasks, which we see through from start to finish, than from repeatedly doing the same small task, or a series of small tasks that do not seem to add up to very much. As the motor industry has discovered, motivation and productivity remains much higher when teams produce complete vehicles, rather than giving individuals mind-numbing and repetitive tasks – which are often more effectively executed by robots.

Communicate purpose – constantly. Many of us hold a mental model of our jobs as just being a set of tasks, rather than a set of tasks with a powerful and guiding purpose behind them. People need to know as much as possible about the purpose behind their jobs, and to be involved in discussion about the appropriateness of the tasks they are being asked to do. And because of widespread unpredictability and uncertainty, the aims of organisations may have to change very quickly. So, again, these changes will need to be communicated. Indeed, a definition of progress in an organisation could be that the higher up you go, the greater the scale of uncertainty you get to deal with . . . Control freaks, bail out now! Lots of tangible examples can help people understand how purpose can shape their decision-making – with instances of how 'rules' may be overturned in order to achieve the greater purpose, say.

Take an example of a shop that has realised it has to be far more innovative to survive and prosper. Its takes on the aim of introducing new approaches wherever possible. The best people to introduce customer-friendly innovation are likely to be those on the shop floor. Traditionally, the managers are meant to have the good ideas, but the best manager in the store introduces a monthly meeting where all rules and practices are to questioned, without any criticism of wacky ideas or schemes. Everyone is encouraged to come along monthly with 'things they would change'. People only incur disapproval for passive unquestioning support of the status quo.

People need to be encouraged to speak up if they are unclear about aspects of their roles and how they relate to its purpose, and to admit to confusion if they are unclear about what their priorities should be. Which brings me neatly to my next point, it's good to . . .

Create an atmosphere of openness and optimism. We human beings are very good at concealing confusion because we want to look good and we don't want to lose face. For there to be really good dialogue going about whether the activities of an organisation are matching its purpose, people have to be encouraged to express their views without being shouted down, punished later or held up to scorn and ridicule.

Cynicism has to be challenged. People usually become cynical as a reaction to having had their hopes dashed in a way that was really hurtful to them. The cynicism becomes a defence mechanism against this ever happening again. An atmosphere of cynicism often develops because disappointment with past failures has not been sufficiently aired. In which case, get a good old whinging session going, and then, after the collective whinge – in the style of a marriage counsellor – insist that all ensuing discussion concentrates on constructive suggestions for the future. All blaming, shaming and recrimination will have been fully exorcised.

Cynics will often rely on 'facts' –whatever they are; some would say 'incontrovertible truths' – to knock down new ideas, dreams and expressions of hope from others. When cynics are being destructively vocal, they need to be asked about their own hopes and dreams, and the constructive suggestions they might offer. You may want to refer back to Chapter Three for more tips on dealing with negaholics.

It's worth noting that there is a difference between cynicism and scepticism: the first tends to be largely destructive, while some sceptical thinking, along the lines of 'Let me consider everything that could possibly go wrong with this scheme', is usually prudent and necessary in most organisational contexts. Take note, too, where a cynic or a sceptic still has a sense of humour. However black, it's an encouraging sign . . . it means they want to stay connected.

Encourage discussion about passion and vision. When we work with others, we need to know what they care about deeply and what engages them fully. We need to know about them personally and to understand, to an extent, their dreams. Sometimes, because of established role-playing, these exchanges have to be semi-formalised.

For example, fairly recently, I've joined the board of a company, and the MD said to me that she would like the board to participate far more in seeking opportunities and networking on behalf of the company. Did I have any ideas about what could be done to encourage this? So I suggested that after the AGM, we each talked a little bit about ourselves and then went on to discuss how we could collectively and actively help the company further. We never got on to the second part of the discussion because despite many of the board members having been in position for four or five years or so, they knew very little about one another. Each person's chat about themselves was interrupted and prolonged as board members discovered all sorts of fascinating things about one another – things of which they had had no previous knowledge. And this isn't some stuffy financial institution, it's a very modern, techi-orientated business, yet people were still revealing very little about themselves *and their potential to work together* in their board member roles.

Now I'm not suggesting that people are given grim little exercises where they all have to sit around and reveal their innermost fantasies, but just giving people opportunities to get to know one another better through encouraging socialising in a relaxed environment, or getting excited collectively at sporting events, can help them establish their shared passions. Once a team is working with shared passion, they have all the motivation they need.

Visions only work when they are collectively created and implemented, and they should represent the goal of the shared passion. The chief executive may have a very powerful vision, but if she's incapable of getting everyone else to be immensely engaged in the decision, then she may as well remain on Planet Zog.

All talk about passion and vision need to be accompanied by lots of plans about action. What do we need to do to make these motivating forces real and tangible?

Recognising meaningfulness

Meaningful work is like a love affair. Intense concentration become easy, we think about our work a great deal, and it simmers away in our unconscious, producing new insights. We borrow time from other distractions to focus on it. Our estimates of what we can produce will be much higher because of our degree of engagement, and we will find obstacles a lot easier to overcome. We will often experience a state called 'flow' (more fully described in my previous book, *Irresistibility*), where we feel entirely absorbed and at one with what we are doing. We are relaxed but energised, and unaware of time pressures.

Unfortunately, many of you, like me, I'm sure, will be all too familiar with the feelings that accompany meaningless work. We get easily distracted, find we can't settle, have a million and one other thoughts in our heads, and somehow find lots of other priorities that crowd in on our time. The work will seem to be piled up in front of us, with the slightest setback taking on a hugely detrimental significance.

Practically meaningful

We can increase meaningfulness for others and ourselves at work through some very practical means:

* Always asking ourselves, 'What are the possibilities in this situation?' as well as asking ourselves, 'What could/is going wrong here?'
* Making sure we *start* the day with things that are most meaningful to us, and leave what we consider to be the less significant tasks to the afternoon.
* Leaving a job when we find ourselves in a situation where our passions and dreams are completely removed. If expediency demands that we stay, we need to acquire very involving hobbies. No one wants to end up living a life of 'quiet desperation'. There is just the one, you know.

Freedom of choice

Our attitudes to choice are shaped by our upbringings. When we are quite small, most of us learn to accept authority from parents, teachers and perhaps elder siblings. As we get older, we often rebel, start to assert ourselves like the young adults we are becoming, and demand to make our own choices. As frequently as possible, these are the opposite of what our parents would want. This is the theory, anyway, though I have to say that we have a six-year-old in our house who's hell-bent on choice sovereignty.

If you work in a burger bar, where you are told you must smile three times at every customer, and end each sale with a 'Have a nice day', your choice options are being very restricted. And, of course, you can sabotage this, smiling in the style of Jack Nicholson in *The Shining* and hissing your 'Have a nice day' through gritted teeth. You are being treated as a child in this role, by an authoritarian employer, and, as such, you have every right in my view to sabotage their instructions by behaving like a naughty one. You will avoid any responsibility because you are not being treated as a responsible adult.

In contrast, in a role where you are clear about your job purpose, and are left to make choices about how to fulfil this job purpose yourself, you will feel very different. You will want to understand as much as you can about the effectiveness of your role, you will know that your opinions and insights matter, and you will feel that you can take initiatives, introduce new practices and experiment. You will have responsibility for how your job is done and what the results are.

Sarah works in human resources in the city of London:

I moved from a big company, which was fairly controlling and authoritarian in its approach to a much smaller one, where I was given the role, a description of what I was supposed to achieve, and then left to find the means to do this. At first, I felt completely at sea, but I knew the company had a very strong sense of flexibility and dynamism, so I leapt in and experimented with a few different approaches. I had to keep communicating like mad with everyone while these experiments were going on, but they all seemed to quite enjoy it. Now we've settled on some systems that suit us and I absolutely love my work – unlike my old company, where everyone focused inwards, I'm really encouraged here to focus outwards all the time in attempts to bring new

> *ideas into the business. I really feel responsible for our*
> *success and that I'm at the heart of things. My confidence in*
> *managing has increased tenfold.*

More choice needed

People who work with you – and you, yourself – may need more choice if you feel any of the following: you feel that you are working too slowly and cannot respond quickly enough to events; you feel that you are being too inflexible to client and customer needs; or you feel that you are not making the most effective use of resources in the organisation.

There will probably need to be discussion about how strong your – and their – commitment is to the purpose behind the tasks, and how able you and they feel to make wise choices. You may need to agree to a trial period where they or you are given more decision-making powers.

Guidelines also need to be established for what happens when the wrong choices are made. John Dewey, the philosopher, was of the view that we do our most potent learning when we are given useful feedback on things that have gone wrong. All parties need to share the view that in decision-making there is very rarely one single best decision: our best stab at good decisions means using all sorts of knowledge – logical, intuitive and tacit – to come up with the best choice within the time frame. People get really good at making choices when they don't feel that a 'wrong' one will blight their careers.

When rules get in the way of allowing people to make decisions, they need to be challenged. A useful question can be, 'Is there any obvious value that prevents me from eliminating this rule?'

Everyone may need to be reminded that in the new economy, a distinguishing feature of top companies will be their ability to attract and keep self-managing people.

Performance and progress

We all love to do things well; it's a massive, motivating buzz. Here are some tips to help others increase their joy in their performance:

Give them encouraging feedback. Tell them frequently and specifically what, in your opinion, they are doing well. And also make constructive suggestions about how their weaker points can improve.

Celebrate their successes. Make public their achievements and organise rewards through events and gifts to highlight these. Recognise both individual and team achievements.

Analyse what's working well. When people are performing well and making progress, it's worth getting their views on what they are doing to get these good results. Although individuals may sometimes be expressing pleasure at what they've achieved, they may put it down to luck, other people's intervention or the task being easy. They may underplay their own contribution and be less likely consciously to develop these skills even further in the future.

Regularly monitor progress. Explain that you wish to increase collaboration, and this involves listening to any concerns they may have. Give time and attention to developing a dialogue and be open about your own concerns.

You can ask for suggestions about how their concerns and your concerns may jointly be met.

Avoid using maths in measuring performance. If goals for the future are predetermined by a mathematical system it is very unlikely to allow for the vagaries of environmental changes. So if you are asked to increase your sales figures by, say, 10 percent every quarter, there will no allowance for the recession that might hit the economy in the last quarter. Unfortunately, maths doesn't predict the future.

Get everyone to meet the customers and clients. Betty in backroom accounts is much more likely to understand the purpose of your business if she meets the people who are at the front end, receiving it. She doesn't have to deal with them on a day-to-day basis, but when she meets them it will make the context in which she works much easier for her to understand. In my experience, too, customers and clients like this sort of involvement, particularly if it involves, wine, women and song . . .

Be critical, but also kind. Perhaps the hardest balance to get right in motivating or, indeed, managing others is how constructively critical of them you are, and also the extent to which you nurture and look after them. The only way to get the balance right is through focusing on them intently, making them comfortable expressing their deeper thoughts and feelings in your company, and being honest with them about how your concern for their wellbeing fits in with your concern for the wellbeing of your organisation.

Now, I'm sure I don't need to tell you this, but all of the above pointers can equally be applied to ourselves. Our own work will motivate us a great deal, when we feel that it is meaningful, that we have freedom of choice in it, and that we are able to monitor our performance and make progress. Looking for every opportunity to create these conditions for others will mean that you motivate them to the fullest degree possible. And from a boss or colleague, we couldn't ask for more.

10 *Wordpower*

'Words are, of course, the most powerful drug used by mankind.'
Rudyard Kipling.

Words are the tools we use to motivate one another. We convey our ideas, our visions and beliefs about others through words. If you're anything like me, you won't spend much time thinking about the words you use in everyday communication: talking face-to-face, on the phone, in e-mail and faxes and – just occasionally these days – the odd letter. And there are times where I wish I had spent more time getting the words absolutely right, in order to convey my meaning – times where people have completely misunderstood what I was getting at, where they have reacted badly to what I thought was just a spirited case, and where I haven't made my true wants nearly clear enough. You see, even we so-called experts don't always get it right.

But being misunderstood and ineffective in communication is not just down to thinking about the use of words. Our use of words is affected by the culture we live in; New Yorkers, for example, will probably be a lot more direct than, say, someone from Buckinghamshire. We'll be affected by how articulate we believe ourselves to be, and the expectations others have of our articulacy. I've often encountered people on courses who stumble and stutter when trying to inspire others – almost entirely because they believed themselves to be 'not very good at it'. And our use of words will be affected by our psychology: common sense dictating to us that if we've been successful in the past through using a certain approach, we will continue to be successful in the future using that approach. Consider Sue's story:

> *I was promoted to MD after having been head of customer relations for five years. I was extremely diplomatic in this role, and good at helping others be so, too. When I took up the MD's role I was shocked by how much more direct I sometimes needed to be – and how much more people expected me to fire from the hip. I got used to it, but sometimes, especially in the first year, I would hear myself being extremely forthright and think 'God, is that really my voice?'*

Great leaders and great careers are often made so by words. Martin Luther King's 'I may not get there with you . . .' may have been put into a dumbed-down context as the backdrop for a television ad, but it still sends tingles up and down my spine when I hear it. At the time of writing, the well-known British barrister, George Carman QC, has just died. In a few pithy phrases, this wordsmith was capable of destroying his victims in court. He memorably described disgraced Tory MP Neil Hamilton as being 'on the make and on the take' while David Mellor – another disgraced Tory – was described as being like 'an ostrich, with his head buried in the sand and his thinking parts exposed'. His use of language was creative and evocative.

So it makes sense, then, that if we want to motivate and inspire others, we use words in as considered a way as we possibly can. In this chapter I analyse different approaches to words and their effects in various contexts. We look at how we can use two very different types of energy to motivate and inspire people. We finish off with a look at the devices of the great and good, and what we can learn from them.

Power behind the words

The words that we use are affected by our power base – that energy and those resources we have that other people may want, admire or find relevant to their lives. In my subject, organisational psychology, 'power' often gets a bad press. It's described as something that people use covertly against one another, and it is built into the deep structure of organisations so that many of us are not aware of its effects. But this risks becoming something of a rather limiting conspiracy theory; and that it's often useful to think of power in more constructive ways. Like money, power itself is a neutral commodity – it's what we do with it that matters, as benevolent despots all over the world know.

The power of powerlessness

The word 'power' holds emotional connotations for many of us. As babies and children, we all knew powerlessness when we relied on others for food, protection and love. We were defined by our parents or parent figures, they told us who we were, and we felt dependant and scared when we thought they had abandoned us, were not looking after our needs, or were angry and cruel to us. If they did not seem to understand us, we would feel confused and anxious.

Some of us make strong associations with fear, deprivation and a loss of control when we hear that word 'power'. People who have it represent a threat to our independence, to our ability to make choices, and to any sense we may have of being able to control people and situations in our own lives. This may make us reactive rather than proactive, because motivating ourselves and taking initiatives involves gaining power. We can't see that power is a means of dealing with fear, of acting and doing to gain control over it. Our sense of powerlessness allows our fears to overwhelm us.

I've no doubt whatsoever that early experiences of power influence how we live our lives. In my own case, having a particularly tyrannical parent who demanded complete control over her children, caused a part of me to become obsessive about my independence and privacy. This manifests itself in odd little ways. For example, I have a fetish for going off on walks in places where no one can find me, and feel great exhilaration at this fact. I just love the feeling that nobody can easily reach me or can pinpoint my whereabouts. Now I've told you, of course, the spell will be broken.

You've got the power . . .

Dictionaries define the word power as the 'ability to do or act'. So while formal title power may be in short supply, through job titles like CEO and MD, there are many different forms of power available. It doesn't have to be a limited resource, which means that if one person has it, others are prevented from having any. Power can be held in very different ways, and often effective personal and professional relationships are built on a delicate see-sawing of power shifts.

Our families may have given us some unhelpful ideas about power – that it is selfish to put our own needs before others, and if we try to get power for ourselves, we will inevitably damage others. This is not a logical cause-and-effect sequence. We may have witnessed examples of power being exercised just by one sex or the other – smothering mother or dominating dad – or received messages that it is 'unfeminine' or 'above our station' to try and make things happen. The use of power in our family may have mainly involved the domination of others without regard to their needs, thoughts and feelings.

But you may have to rethink somewhat your definitions of power. It is possible to power share, without others taking advantage of this. Your personal power, the capacity you have as a human being to make things happen, is likely to be considerable. In situations where your ability to motivate is critical, an analysis of your power base should prove very helpful. You may find it helpful to ask yourself the following questions:

- Do you have any formal authority?
- What rules and procedures can you operationalise as a result of this?
- Do you control anything that is in scarce supply; for example, money, creativity, opportunities, tact and diplomacy, or historical knowledge about the ways things work in your organisation?
- Do you control access to anything?
- To what extent are you able to cope with uncertainty?
- Who do you know who makes you well-connected?
- Over what are you able to take decisions?
- About what do you have knowledge and information that is valuable?
- How good are you at engaging others and getting them to collaborate with you?
- To what emotions are you effective at appealing in others?

Your answers will identify the specific power resources you hold. You may find it helpful to write them down to remember them. This is an exercise that can't be rushed: the questions require some thinking to answer.

While you may not want to make explicit what you consider your power resources over others to be, clearly identifying them for yourself before attempting to motivate others will help you be more effective.

Now let's go on to optimise your use of power through words and an analysis of different effects.

The motivational push

Successfully using words is helpful when you want to be up and at people. The energy behind using words to best effect is a strong thrusting one, and you will feel as though you are moving towards people. There are two different approaches here:

A logical appeal

This involves putting forward ideas, suggestions and proposals, and backing them up with reasons. Along the lines of: 'We might like to think of . . . and the reasons for this are', 'I'd like to suggest . . . because . . . (subsequent reasons)', or 'This is happening, this is happening, and this is happening, and for these reasons I suggest we . . .'

You'll probably already use this approach if you go to lots of meetings, where you enjoy making suggestions and arguing cases that appeal to the logic and rationality of others present. You may be less comfortable using this approach if you feel apprehensive about expressing your ideas to others, and lack confidence about making a case.

If you lack confidence in your self-image as a rational, logical human being, then again you may shy away from expressing a suggestion like this.

Most cases in meetings start with a logical appeal and often move on to something stronger. To use this logical appeal effectively your opinions and analysis have to be taken seriously by others. In other words, you have to have expert power.

And because expert power tends to be more highly valued among groups of people who hold the expertise in common: if you are trying to motivate a group of your peers then you will probably use a logical appeal more often than if you were talking to a group of people who did not have this expertise in common.

But a logical appeal can be limited in trying to motivate others, because some argumentative types will interpret any reasoned argument as an invitation to counter-reason. Furthermore, it is purely limited to a 'head' appeal. When I describe this approach to motivating people to GPs, they often make comments like: 'Some patients follow courses of treatment given sufficient reason, but others need something stronger.'

And those of us who love reasoning can find ourselves, if we are not careful when using the logical approach, getting into our twenty-seventh reason for doing something – failing to notice that our motivational targets are all deeply comatose . . .

Gareth is a civil servant:

In the civil service we use logic and reasoning a great deal. We all tend to be educated to value these processes and also to view ourselves as aids to ministers in using these processes. But sometimes because we are being so polite and

> *rational, the message just doesn't get through. I always remind newcomers in my department of the way in which submariners in the USA are trained to speak to their commanders with a: 'Sir, it is my duty to inform you that if we do not change course we will collide with that vessel'. There are times, I suggest, when ministers may need that direct an approach if they are to heed our advice.*

Sometimes people use a logical approach because they are more comfortable with rather indirect communication. So Sue will say to Lavinia who works with her, 'Lavinia, I suggest you improve the way you speak to clients, because three have complained in the past month and it isn't in keeping with our ethos.' But what Sue really means is: 'Lavinia, you'd better change your attitude towards our clients if you want to keep working here.'

Using the logical approach creates a gentle push to motivate people and often sounds like an invitation to enter into debate. If this falls on deaf ears, you may need move to something stronger, like:

A forceful appeal

This approach is much more direct, and it involves stating what you want or need, evaluating the situation, and offering a carrot and stick to motivate people. So it's along the lines of: 'I need you to change this; you are doing A well, but B needs some improvement. If you improve the way you deal with B, I can see a pay rise on the horizon, but if you don't, I can't.'

You'll probably already use this approach if you are assertive, if you are accustomed to letting others know what you expect from them, are comfortable instructing, praising and criticising others, and find it easy to put pressure on other people. You may need to increase your use of this technique if you don't like using the 'I' word, if you think you frequently appear indecisive and sub-missive, if you can't say no, and if you avoid conflict and compromise too readily. In other words, if you feel others regard you as a wimp and a pushover, this is the approach you'll need to take.

This technique is particularly useful when people need to understand very clearly the rewards and downsides of different courses of action. It is often helpful when a situation is hurtling towards a crisis. For example, 'I suggest we leave the building and there are a couple of reasons for this. One is that the fire brigade seem to be trying to force entry and the second is that . . .' will not be as effective as 'I want us to leave. The building's on fire. If we leave, we live, if we don't, we won't'. Point made, I think.

It helps to have some sort of legitimate authority or title-power when using this approach. Generally speaking, we are more likely to accept ultimatums from the prime minister, president, CEO or head consultant then we are from Lavinia in accounts. But if you don't have this power, then it is vital to be clear about what you resources you do control, and what you can genuinely reward and threaten people with.

Colin is an operations manager:

> I've always regarded myself as a direct, plain speaker but I often feel awkward in meetings. and that's because I think I raise the emotional temperature with too hectoring a tone. I am training myself to be a bit more tentative in the interests of diplomacy, asking more questions, taking other people's

> *opinions and just making mild suggestions, rather than taking strong stands on issues. Everyone knows though, they can really on me to take a stand when needed!*

When people use forceful appeals too often, they may appear coercive and autocratic. Now nobody likes a bully and at some stage, even if the forceful member of the group has a lot of legitimate authority, those on the receiving end of this approach will at some level scatter. Ruling through fear almost always involves people retreating and launching protests through covert means. In organisational life, that manifests itself as behavioural problems, such as poor time-keeping, absenteeism, 'forgetting' to mention important information, and doing absolutely no more than the minimum the job description requires.

For the person who is not comfortable standing up for him or herself, then this is an approach that is best rehearsed at home – aloud – before delivering it for real. You will minimise the sense of shock you feel when you express your views.

The motivational pull

This way of employing words to best effect is appropriate to use when you want people to engage strongly in your vision and ideas, and it will help you to put them into practice. It involves using emotional intelligence: thinking hard about people's feelings and reactions to your initiatives. Again, there are two different approaches here:

The participative appeal

This involves listening, involving and disclosing – in their purest forms – which is, of course, one of the mainstays of counselling. But don't worry – I'm not trying to turn you into a funny-looking bloke with a small dark beard, who strokes his beard reflectively, while saying: 'very interesting' at their clients' every utterance. No, this is simply a useful approach to motivating others that may help them and you understand what's blocking their motivation.

You'll probably already be comfortable using this approach if you ask people for their opinions and suggestions – and listen carefully to their responses – if you are fairly open with your thoughts, feelings and intentions, and if you bring in people who are isolated. You will find it helpful to become more comfortable with this approach if you frequently try to control and dominate people and situations, if you fail to notice others' concerns, or if you suspect you come over as 'too pushy' or 'a cold fish'.

Participation is particularly useful when you want to research anything: how much people know about a situation and how strongly they feel about it, or what people's initial reactions are to your new initiative. It's also helpful when you suspect people are uncomfortable or unsure about how they really feel and may be concealing their true emotions. It's worth remembering that when we really feel strongly about something, our powers of articulacy often plummet drastically. We literally get a 'lump in the throat', which may prevent us speaking.

This approach requires what I like to call 'humanity power'. It's the ability to connect with others, to make them feel comfortable with you, and to trust you. You only exude this power if you have true integrity: just going through the motions, nodding, smiling and saying, 'I hear what you say' won't work at all. Even the most innocent of us can sniff inauthenticity a mile away – just watch three-year-olds respond to someone they don't trust.

Disclosure can benefit from being timely and appropriate. If you're giving people complex information, then revealing that you found the information quite hard to assimilate yourself will make them feel better. But divulging your entire family history and the trauma it caused you will just make them feel embarrassed. Anyway, you wouldn't be so daft, would you?

This approach – genuinely listening and identifying with others – has not traditionally been accepted in old-style macho management and approaches to motivation. And there are still people in organisational positions of power who are actually incapable of asking the most potent of open questions: 'What do you think?' Instead, they have to rephrase their query as, 'This is what I think; don't you agree?' Fortunately, in these times of networking and coaching, these dinosaurs are becoming extinct.

Too much of this approach though can have its downsides. I always imagine, rather stereotypically, a group of counselling psychologists trying to reach a decision about something. Everyone constantly asks, 'How do you feel?' and 'What are your responses to this?' All involved have a great and good therapeutic dump of their feelings, and five hours later no course of action has been agreed . . .

When you are trying to motivate a group of people within a short time-span, then it's important to make your use of the participative approach a timely one. Use it extensively early on in the proceedings, to deal with any underlying concerns and feelings, and you should have a smoother ride a bit later. If, on the other hand, you allow feeling and concerns to build up and remain unexpressed, and then embark on a lot of participation, you may find it extremely difficult to push through your agenda.

The inspirational approach

This approach involves identifying common ground and creating a vision. It runs along the lines of: 'So we all agree, I think, that we could work more effectively around here. Picture this, not only are we working more efficiently but also feeling much more involved and fulfilled at work. We really feel like our contribution matters.'

You'll already be using this approach if you frequently unite people for a shared cause, if you readily convey enthusiasm and optimism to others, and are described as 'visionary' and 'inspiring'. You'll find it useful to become better at using this approach if you find it very difficult to express zeal and enthusiasm, if you expect things to go wrong a lot of the time, and regard yourself as 'unimaginative'.

The inspirational approach is essential when you want to motivate people over a period of time. When I was advising on the last election campaign, I ran a workshop for campaign organisers on how to motivate volunteers. They knew they were in for a long haul with these volunteers, that they would be asking them to stuff many tens of thousands of envelopes, and that quite a few people become political volunteers because of social isolation. Many of the organisers knew, too, that just setting endless targets to these volunteers didn't work as a motivational tactic. Instead, we broadened our discussion to encompass what it was that volunteers got out of helping with political campaigns. The organisers came up with answers like, 'sense of belonging', 'sense of being a part of something much bigger', and 'really feeling significant if we win'. They concluded that their two biggest motivational tools were praise and recognition – and lots of it for individual effort – and repeated reminders about the fantastic party that would celebrate victory on election night. And, of course, that party really happened.

When we identify common ground with others, it's important not to make assumptions. The company chairman who announced to a disaffected workforce that, 'We all want to make the company profitable' may be assuming that the top wishes of the shareholders are very similar to those of the workers. Very often we will need to check that our ideas about common ground are truly representative; yes, the best way to do that is through some participation. Identifying and describing common ground is a diplomatic tactic; it shows that we are considering the viewpoints of the people we are hoping to motivate.

It's best not to create a vision that sounds like you are living on the planet Zog while the rest of us are on planet Earth. But visions must have a element of flight and fantasy about them: they are, after all, appeals to the imagination. And because the imagination is such a potent force in motivating us, if the vision hits the collective needs and fantasies of those particular people at that particular time and in those particular circumstances – as Martin Luther King, Hitler, Margaret Thatcher, Bill Clinton and Tony Blair learned – then you are on to a winner. In more mundane instances, we very often find that a canny visionary gets themselves a right-hand pragmatist, who can calm any doubts that the visionary is off into orbit. For example, in the UK, our rather visionary leader, Tony Blair, has a dour pragmatic right-hand chancellor in Gordon Brown.

To use the inspirational approach very effectively, people have got to believe that you have integrity behind your mission, and that this integrity will motivate you to deliver on your promises. You need a kind of charismatic power that will convince people it is safe to entrust you with their hopes, and that you will build on them.

Janice is in the retail business:

> When I started being a manager about ten years ago, we were still very much regarded in this business as people who controlled and monitored the staff. Things have certainly changed now, and we are increasingly being told we must motivate and coach. I was worried about this – I never learned how to motivate on any courses – and I went and saw our head of training. He sent me on a programme on persuasive communication, where I learned about telling stories, about using case histories and examples, about drawing parallels from everyday life with business models, that people would understand. I was videoed making a case and everyone seemed to think I had considerable powers of motivation.

Avoiding motivation

There are times where it may be wiser to delay motivating people. When they're exhausted, depressed or even elated, you may be better off waiting until their mood is calmer. It will be easier to predict what you need to do in these circumstances.

Techniques of the Great and Good

Charismatic behaviour has two distinctive qualities. The speaker appears to have a strong sense of mission and purpose. They will appear extremely enthusiastic and committed. But this is balanced by an evident sense of caring about the audience, about building a connection with them, and about endorsing the speaker's relationship with the audience. In short, a balance of will and warmth.

When we analyse memorable rhetoric, we see it is structured around certain devices. These are:

Comparison and contrast. In other words, how things are the same and how things are different. This is fundamental to the way we process the world; we sort out when we are very small that mum is different from dad, that day is different from night, that sweet is different from sour. So whenever we receive any sort of information, we filter it according to what it reminds us of, and what it is different from. In other words, we rely on associations.

In that well-known speech, Martin Luther King says:

> I may not get there with you
> But I want you to know tonight
> That we as a people will get to the promised land

Lists of three. Brains assimilate information best in a small number of chunks. And we understand patterns best if they are in odd numbers, rather than evens. So, very often lists of three form a considerable part of inspirational speaking:

> So I'm happy tonight
> I'm not worried
> I'm not fearing any man . . .

Repetition. On the basis that if you are trying to inspire a lot of people, and many of them may not be listening that well, key messages need to be repeated, repeated and repeated. As UK Prime Minister Tony Blair proclaimed when he first came to office, his priority was to be: 'Education, education, education'.

Words and behaviour

Words do not stand alone, of course; they are delivered in a certain tone of voice, with a facial expression, body language, in a specific context and with others present (or not). If the chips are down, you are desperate to get through to someone, lose your temper, and appear angry while trying to use the logical approach in words, you'll create confusion and conflict. On the other hand, if you behave in a calm and controlled manner, while issuing a direct ultimatum through the forceful approach, your message is far more likely to hit home.

Ultimately, behaviour is as important as words, and the next chapter will focus on just that. We'll look at how to appear inspiring, sound inspiring and spread inspiration. The result? You'll be even better at motivating, motivating, motivating.

11 Inspiring Behaviour

'Only fools don't judge by appearances.'
Oscar Wilde

When I have the time, I like to think long and hard before I write each chapter of a book. And when I was preparing this chapter, I started to think about people I regarded as being inspiring. One person in particular came to mind: a friend of mine. She is not well-known and she will remain anonymous for the purposes of discretion. She is a teacher and a coach and she is utterly inspiring to many people who come into contact with her. I have watched her work a great deal, and she never fails to make me – and I'm only in an observer's role – feel good.

So how does this friend of mine achieve this miraculous feat? Well, she is not very well-educated or articulate – indeed, at times, and especially when she is travelling the realms of the abstract, she can talk complete and utter garbage. Her sentences will meander and be non-sequential, yet most people present will grasp at some phrases and get the gist of what she is on about. And she will remain powerfully persuasive and inspirational, even when it is quite difficult to follow her meaning.

I decided that there was a lot I could learn from my friend and – surprise, surprise – when I analysed her behaviour, she shared a lot in common with people who are much more celebrated than she is. Her overwhelming characteristics are commitment to people and enthusiasm for what she does. You can't feel these qualities if you're over-concerned about yourself and how others are thinking about you. You have to getupandgrow out of this.

In this chapter, I want to look at how we inspire others through our behaviour signals, and how we look and sound, and how to inspire others when we feel demotivated ourselves. My friend is a goddess of emotional contagion – the emotion being enthusiasm. Here's how you can pass on the bug to others, too.

The appearance of enthusiasm

Probably one of the few rules that regularly applies to humans is that behaviour breeds behaviour. If you look enthusiastic and keen to be talking to people, they are far more likely to reciprocate with openness and energy. And we know that in situations where people are trying to influence one another, and power is fairly evenly distributed between them, then it will be the most expressive person who is likely to influence the other's mood.

Let's analyse some of the signals that convey enthusiasm:

Movement with a purpose

Karen Horney was a psychoanalyst who said humans could only move in three directions in our dealings with others: towards others, against them, or away from them. Inspiring behaviour is about moving towards others. When people move with energy, purpose and other directed attention, they are much more likely to inspire others.

Some of you may be thinking of people who walk into a room so full of energy that they appear hypermanic and scary, or hugely attention-seeking, rather than exhibiting a desire to connect to others. The sort of energy I'm talking about here is controlled, and suggestive of someone who is capable of being both proactive and receptive.

And how do we get this flow of energy? Well, through good connections with our own bodies, through understanding where we take tension and how to relieve it, and tuning into our fluctuating reserves of the stuff. Here are some insights from Maria:

> I always have thought of myself as an enormously energetic person. My parents were like that and everyone in our family does lots and throws themselves into life with gusto. After I had my first baby, I went into total shock about this aspect of myself. Yes, OK, I'd been tired while pregnant, but the physical lulls were always accompanied by a huge amount of excitement about pregnancy and my baby. But just after the birth – sleep deprived and both physically and mentally shattered, even to the point of my previously razor-sharp memory not seeming to function at all – I experienced, for the first time in thirty-four years, complete and utter exhaustion. I had always viewed myself as having unlimited reserves of energy, and suddenly I realised that I had to view it differently – as something I took care of and rationed, grabbing sleep whenever I could and expending energy only on my topmost priorities.

I don't think this means we need to be precious about our energy levels, just that we can't always expect it to be there in huge reserves, and whenever we need it. During periods where we are experiencing lots of physical and/or psychological change, we are bound to find things more difficult.

Tension checks

I'm sure most of you are self-aware enough to realise that the body and mind are a system, and when you are under pressure, tension will manifest itself in different parts of the body. Consistently scrunching up in one place – and I mean mentally or physically – can result in tension and pain manifesting itself elsewhere. There is no new-age mystique about this, folks; there are nerve receptors in cells located around the body that respond to emotional change. And I'm fairly certain that we have an intuitive knowledge of this – why else would we talk about someone being 'a pain in the neck' or having 'a lump in the throat' or 'shouldering too much responsibility'.

Alexander Technique, which teaches correct posture, alignment and using the body, and Pilates, a focusing and freeing gentle exercise system, are excellent ways to learn how we hold and release tension from our bodies. And there's more. If you can find a therapy or discipline, whether it's yoga, martial arts or even massage, that helps you to cope with tension, and to learn to use your body in more effective, tension-releasing ways, there's no doubt but that you'll benefit in the long-term. Furthermore, you'll be enhancing your greatest natural resource: energy!

Revving up

When you're going somewhere with the purpose of inspiring people; it's worth checking tension spots beforehand. We tend to take tension in our jaws, facial muscles, necks, shoulders, abdomen and knees. So a quick warm-up with a few yawns to stretch and relax the face, a few gentle nods of the head to relax the neck, some shoulder rolls and shrugs to release those shoulders, easy breaths low in the lungs to release the abdomen out as the breath drops in and a quick shake of the legs will all help.

You are much more likely to feel inspired and inspiring

yourself if you feel warmed up, and with a good strong circulation. So before any crucial motivational encounter, get yourself down the gym, go for a run or swim, or do five minutes of exercises to get those inspirational juices flowing. It's worth bearing in mind, too, that if you feel in the slightest way nervous or apprehensive, those warmed-up muscles do not vibrate in the same way that cold muscles do. Your warmed-up muscles will be far more responsive to messages from the brain that say things like 'relax' and 'look pleased to be here'.

With no luxury of time to do this, warm yourself up through walking to work, using the stairs rather than the lift, and taking breaks as quick trots around the block rather than a collapse in the coffee bar.

Body positioning

When your aim is to inspire people, you don't want to hang around the periphery of anywhere. You literally want to look like you want to get 'stuck in'. So sit and stand right in the centre of a room, where everyone can see that you are there with a strong central sense of purpose.

If you're standing or sitting opposite an individual or several people, you want to look leader-like, which means taking up plenty of space, while maintaining good posture. No hunching or apologetic tilt of the chin downwards, please. You will find rapport with others increases if you use body language that reflects theirs. This doesn't mean exact mimicry, but if they are slouched down in their chairs, for example, you can relax back more into yours. Avoid reacting to their style, by sitting purposefully erect. Always my favourite word, that last one, when it comes to talking about body language.

Fixing that face

How do you look enthusiastic? Well, my friend and colleague, Chris Kelly, always gets people to try and 'twinkle' through their facial expression. Sometimes just mentioning that fairylike word so disarms people (whose self-images have never, ever allowed them to twinkle in their entire lives) that for a moment, they do. He wants his clients to lighten up, to convey a sense of playfulness, to look like they are having fun. This is his advice: Relax those facial muscles through performing the following sequence. Drop the tongue so it rests behind the bottom teeth, open the mouth slightly and think about smiling with the eyes, so the cheek muscles lift slightly; breathe out gently. There, you're twinkling! Not a manic grin, but a very engaging twinkle which can be perfected to order.

Inspiring eyes

If there's just one message you get from this entire book, I'd like it to be that motivating others is all about connecting with them. As you've probably guessed, this makes it pretty important to look at them when you meet them, and when you talk and listen to them. You can't motivate others – unless it's through very short-term coercive fear – by ignoring them. The more you look at people as they respond to what you've suggested, the more you can pick up on all their feelings and thoughts about your ideas – even the unspoken ones. This doesn't mean staring, just a great deal of attentiveness, concentrating on the other person's agenda rather than your own.

Great orators from history, such as Enoch Powell, General Patton and Tony Benn, have usually had very expressive or piercing eyes. If you wear make-up, then you might want to emphasise your eyes, especially if you're making a presentation that you aim to make inspirational. For the same reason, if you can avoid wearing tinted glasses in this context, so much the better.

Clothes that boost

Most of us regard clothes as something that gives us a boost. And, of course, clothing has qualities that make us feel good – think about the cosiness of cashmere, or the sensuality of silk – but have no effect on onlookers. But if we're going to motivate and inspire others, there are some guidelines we can use to achieve best effect by what we wear:

Warm colours 'advance' towards people and cool colours retreat. Black absorbs energy, and white reflects it. The colour you choose to place next to your face is the most important colour. I notice that my aforementioned friend always looks shiny: she wears white collars near her face, shiny jewellery and her face has a glow, which, knowing her lifestyle, I suspect is cosmetically created, rather than anything to do with antioxidants from fruit and veg.

In chapter nine I talked about how human beings need structure and tasks. If we're trying to inspire others, we can reflect this through a sense of 'togetherness' in our appearance. I don't mean tailored clothes, necessarily, which in a lot of contexts can look quite old-fashioned, but rather an attention to detail that indicates thoughtfulness and thoroughness that your audience may find contagious.

It makes sense, too, to draw attention to your best points. If you've got what you regard as inspiring breasts or pecs, then let them be seen. I'm not suggest you leap into the boardroom looking like Pamela Anderson or Arnie Schwarzenegger, but, hey, it could be just what that dull as semolina board meeting needs. I'm calling for letting others see the suggestion of the pneumatic or the pumped under that fine wool sweater. You've gotta use all you've got baby.

The sound of enthusiasm

Many of us find the workings of our voices somewhat mysterious: we know we'd like to sound enthusiastic, but we don't want to end up sounding like an over-excited children's television presenter. Fortunately for us, voice technique is highly scientific, which means that different voice effects can be explained. So if you want to sound inspiring try the following:

Keeping it pacey

A plodding delivery won't inspire anyone – not even the most nervous of listeners – so we need to keep the pace cracking along. But sometimes, when people get carried away with their enthusiasm, they start to breathe rapidly and audibly in the top part of the chest, snatching in breaths. If you do this for any length of time, you will start to hyperventilate, which is taking the cause of inspiration much too far.

By all means, keep the words coming out briskly, but do check that when you pause for breath, you let that breath drop easily into the bottom part of the lungs in an effortless way. You won't lose your enthusiasm and you'll remain clearly conscious – a plus in most circumstances.

Moving those lips

Consonants are created by the speech organs, the jaw, tongue, teeth and lips. And consonants sound the structural elements of words, contrasted with vowels which carry the emotional elements. So to sound bright and crisp, those lips need to move quite energetically. You can experiment with this thesis if you like: read a sentence drawing out all the vowels, and then read one really crisply enunciating the consonants. If you record yourself and play it back, you'll notice a big difference. Thinking of Noel Coward in the second instance can be helpful. If you take a wildly over-enunciated delivery, and then pull it back to something that's just a wee bit more crisp and energetic than usual, you should be approaching the inspirational.

Pitching up

We all have pitch patterns in our speech, and our range of pitch is often determined by accent. We Celts often sound more inspirational than people from the South of England, because our accents travel over a wider range of notes.

Celtic or not, when we get enthusiastic we often use more pitch rises in the middle of sentences and on words that are particularly interesting. Try talking and just raising your finger occasionally to get a pitch lift if you feel you sound too downbeat.

Playing your instrument

There are lots of ways of freeing up your voice to make it sound more expressive. Just singing a bit more at home, in the privacy of the bathroom – or in the office if you want to lose friends and demoralise people – can help you enjoy your sound more. I think you *have* to have a slight element of enjoying your own voice to really inspire people, without slipping over into a self-reverential tone.

It can also help to listen to famous speeches and to imitate their style. Have fun parodying, 'We will fight them on the beaches' (Churchill). But don't do a William Hague, *pleeeaase?* I think someone has suggested to him that he listen to Martin Luther King, who had a uniquely individual, almost intoning style of delivery, which transferred beautifully from pulpit to podium. William Hague attempts to intone slightly, hoping I think that we will find it hypnotic. But, sorry, to my ears, it just sounds downright daft, Will.

Do some analysis of your own speaking style. Record yourself talking about a great passion, such as a sexual fetish, chocolate or wind-surfing. You can be as vivid as you like, because no one else is going to hear it. Then go on to talk about something you would like to motivate others to do or to think differently about. Do the two styles sound very different? Can you put elements of the first into the second? This is a particularly useful exercise if you are going to make an inspirational presentation. Concentrate on getting the opening sounding really upbeat and attention-grabbing. Here's Simon's experience:

> I've always had a really boring voice, which isn't helped by the fact that I'm an accountant. I've always dreaded the annual report presentation, as I see my audience yawning in expectation when I come into the room. Anyway, when I was promoted to finance director, my wife suggested that I did something about my voice. She booked me in with a drama teacher, which I found really mortifying to begin with, but then I really began to enjoy it. I learned all about how the voice works, and how to use mine more expressively. She had me reading Shakespeare and Winnie the Pooh, and I loved it all. I started to get much bolder in my approach to presenting, and to use a lot more theatrical elements.

I started to regard the whole thing as fun – completely aside from my efficacy in the role of FD. Someone told me the other day that my reports are now the highlight of annual conference – nobody knows what to expect or what devices might be used. And because I really sound like I'm enjoying it, they do too. I still think my natural inclination is to sound boring – I like order and control so much – but changing my attitude to the whole thing big-time has really helped.

Motivating others when you feel demotivated

Make no bones about it, this is difficult. But there are lots of occasions in life where this particular skill is demanded of us – when we head a team in work that has a suffered a big setback, when our children are upset at failure and we feel under the weather ourselves, when a partner's been made redundant, and we feel utterly exhausted. I could go on, but my aim is to inspire not depress. Instead, here are some tips for summoning up the energy to motivate when you'd rather be in bed:

Visualise yourself in top form

We need to use the mind's eye, that most potent of motivators, in these circumstances. Just take a few minutes, where you know you will be undisturbed, to relax and close your eyes. Think of a situation where you felt yourself to be in top form, and replay it in your mind. Really enjoy watching yourself feeling energetic and enthusiastic. See other people who were there really being inspired by your enthusiasm and enjoying your energy.

Sandwich your task between treats

When you are feeling under par and in desperate need of some tender loving care yourself, you really must attend to these needs, too. So if you're landed with the task of motivating someone else, try and sandwich it between a couple of treats for yourself. Start yourself with a really yummy breakfast, for instance, get on with the job, and that evening have a truly luxurious bath with candles, oil and the lot. If you can't do both, then at least have the bath; the subsequent treat is the most important one, because having planned it, it will minimise any feelings you may have about 'What about me?' or 'This is really unfair that I have to keep giving like this'. When you're feeling ill or tired, it's really important to pamper yourself a great deal afterwards, and to plan the treats in advance of your presentation.

Check that your feelings about this are situation specific

Is this is one-off response to having to motivate others? Is your apathy caused by the specifics of the situation? Or, are you feeling like this as part of a more general feeling of 'Poor old me, the dogsbody'? If you are absolutely honest with yourself and know it to be a response that is part of a more general feeling, then you need to set aside some time to concentrate on finding what the Americans call more 'me-time'.

Wear something that makes you feel really good

If you've got a stinking cold and you'd really like to wear your cashmere cardigan rather than a suit, then I'd say: What the hell, wear that cardie and explain away your casual garb through drawing attention to your red nose and regular sneezing . . .

Focus on the other person/people completely

However you feel, when you are trying to inspire another party, it's important to focus on them completely. Before you meet them, remind yourself what it is they need and want from you and which of their best interests you are serving. Keep your meeting shortish and very focused on their responses, and make sure that you repeatedly point out what is in it for them.

Explain to people if your symptoms are obvious

This doesn't mean using excuses, or sounding apologetic, but if you are suffering disappointment, ill-health or exhaustion, then it is worth reminding people that you are only human, too. Some of us have a 'be-strong' tendency, which means that we feel we are very responsible, that we can run things better than anyone else, and that the buck always stops with us. As a result, we can be poor at delegating, poor at asking others for help, and regarded by others as 'a tough old boot who can stand on her own two feet'. We may regularly conceal our own feelings, so that others begin to believe that we simply haven't got any. Through creating a strong exterior, we may be treating ourselves very cruelly on the inside, and allowing others to deny that we have feelings, too. We may forget, if we're leading a disappointed team, for instance, that they would feel better if they saw us expressing similar feelings to the ones they are experiencing.

When people have a very strong 'be-strong' tendency, they very rarely ask or get any help until they collapse in spectacular style. Don't let this happen to you. Life's too short to spend any of it in the throes of a nervous breakdown.

Concentrate on the task in hand

View your task as a short but important one, and a job that needs to be done as well as you can under the circumstances. This is not a time to reflect upon your universal shortcomings as an individual, or to be overly concerned about what people think about you. Concentrate on getting through the task, without worrying too much about relationships. This doesn't mean be insensitive – of course you need to consider people's feelings beforehand and during your chat – but your *top* priority should be achieving the task that's required. Postpone any relationship negotiations for a time when you feel stronger.

And if you're having to motivate the demotivated over a period of time?

Roger is a manager in an internet company, and he had an interesting experience:

> Shortly before Christmas last year, we knew that some of us were going to be laid off. At the same time we had some really big projects that had to be finished before the end of the year, about which people needed to remain motivated. I really felt for all my team – they were working in an atmosphere of both pressure and great uncertainty – and I had to keep them motivated. I deliberately created a live-for-today attitude, was completely open about the degree of uncertainty with which we were working, but chivvied everyone on to do their best on a daily basis. We went out a lot after work to the pub, and really made the most of the camaraderie that was in the team. The lay-offs, when they came, were much less than expected and we only lost a couple of people – who seemed quite happy to get

pay-offs anyway. Over Christmas, I realised that I had been acting a quite relentless cheeriness for several weeks, and I felt really run down. So I treated myself and the family to a last-minute break in the sun in the New Year. Everything is on a more even keel now, but I think my tactics on the whole worked and I would use them again in similar circumstances.

So stay short-term and relationship-centred in your thinking, while being aware of what the situation is doing to you, and rewarding yourself afterwards.

Now we positive-thinking types avoid the word 'problem', so in this last chapter let's move onto something that many of us find a 'challenge': motivating family and friends.

12 *Family and Friends*

A few years ago, someone close to me went into hospital for a minor surgical procedure. Unexpectedly, they haem-orrhaged during the procedure and ended up in intensive care. I've visited very sick people before, but when I saw this person I was very shocked indeed. I had always viewed him as a really strong individual, both physically and mentally, and to see him partially conscious, vulnerable and heavily dependant on medical equipment was really startling.

And that's the type of experience that can occur when we are called upon to motivate people who are very close to us. We suddenly have to re-evaluate our view of them: to help them through a cycle of change that may knock the stuffing out of them, and to help them pick themselves us again. And while all this change is happening, they may become unrecognisable to us as the people we knew, that our relationship will need to readjust accordingly.

In this chapter, then, we look at how we can help re-motivate partners, children and friends. Let's start with partners:

Inspiring a demotivated partner

Something we human beings tend to do a great deal is to assume that others, especially our partners, will and should react in the same way that we do. So if a partner is made redundant, stricken with illness or passed over with promotion, we assume that they should do exactly what we would do in those circumstances: get job searching at 8am every morning, bombard ourselves with alternative remedies, or start networking like mad in order to get into another department. But in making this assumption we overlook the fact that each one of us is utterly unique and that however empathic we regard ourselves as being, we cannot truly live any experience for another person.

It's worth thinking about what individuals experience as they go through change. Elizabeth Kubler-Ross, a doctor, wrote a marvellous book with the cheery title, *On Death and Dying*. I describe it as 'marvellous' because it really is an amazingly inspiring portrait of how the terminally ill handle their prognosis. The author describes stages that the patients go through: denial and isolation, anger, bargaining, depression and acceptance. These stages can co-exist alongside one another at the same time. More interestingly, perhaps, these stages are still identifiable when people are experiencing less significant change.

Denial and isolation. This is a game we often play, pretending that whatever it is that is affecting us just isn't happening. So your partner's business may be in trouble, but she blithely continues shopping, spending and going to work with gusto until the accountant forces her to sit down and take note of what is happening. Then she may well start to feel isolated, with a sense of injustice. We've all experienced this, I think – that sense of 'How on earth could this happen to me?'

Anger. A sense of disbelief is often followed by anger. And this anger may not be directed at the real source of what's happened, which is often fate, anyway. Instead, your partner may get angry with you and with the children, if you have any, as you are easy and available targets. In truth, however, they are really angry about the injustice done to them, and having to put their plans on hold.

Bargaining. As children we often learn that bargaining works. Tidying our room regularly, for instance, can result in an increase in pocket money. So, as adults, we often try the same sort of tactic, thinking, 'If I put a huge amount of effort into job search and start at 8am every morning, I am *bound* to be rewarded with a new job within six months.' Shame is, life isn't that straightforward, and it certainly isn't as fair. While putting huge efforts into a job search is more likely to result in a new job, it sadly does not guarantee it.

Depression. In *On Death and Dying*, Dr Kubler Ross discusses two types of depression: preparatory depression is caused by impending death, while reactive depression has more to do with responses and concerns about the changes that are occurring. A demotivated partner who is suffering from reactive depression to change may benefit greatly from knowing that whatever has been taken away from them in one context, remains in another. If they are missing feeling powerful at work, then achieving some power in the community may be helpful; if people relied on them in a business, then reminding them how much they are relied on at home may be helpful; if they were once physically strong, then reminding how strong they are in their parenting skills may be a good boost.

Acceptance. This is a stage where people do not have particularly strong feelings. They are resigned to what has happened and reconciled to living with it. When un-welcome change hits us, many of us benefit from help in venting anger, envy and resentment to accept what has happened and move on.

Helping with change

Here are some practical tips:

- If your partner is behaving strangely during a period of turbulent change, ask yourself what they might be experiencing, according to the different stages. Talk to them about this if you feel it would be appropriate.
- Don't feel that you need relentlessly to cheer up a depressed partner. Sometimes, they may be better off being left to wallow in their gloom for a while, however hard it may be for you to witness. It may help them through an important transition.
- Ask yourself, 'To what extent can I influence my partner's moods and responses?' 'Am I giving sufficient attention to my own well-being too?'

Here's Kathryn's experience:

Henry, my partner, has had a disastrous few years professionally. He was made redundant once, then he ran a small business which failed, then two years later he was made redundant again. His industry has been going through dramatic change and only really big corporations are surviving in it. He was never fortunate enough to be employed by one of these. After the second redundancy I was really worried about him. He usually copes with change by becoming very proactive and busy, but this time he announced that he was just going to holiday for a while. He said that we'd have to tighten our belts while he took a break to sort himself out. I knew the cumulative effect of all this change had left him exhausted, but I wasn't prepared for this reaction. I thought he'd gone mad. Anyway he took a three-month break, getting up late, pottering at home, cooking and picking up the kids from school, and then threw himself back into the job search. He was refreshed and revitalised and got a job with one of those big corporations. I'll trust his instincts more in future.

Relationship expectations

When change affects your partner, you may feel upset on their behalf by what has happened. However, more significantly, you may be upset by the fact that your expectations were not met. A friend whose husband has a degenerative illness is sadder about not being able to enjoy an active retirement together than she is about him getting the illness in the first place. Our expectations may include ideas like: she/he will look after me, we will share interests together, we will have the holiday of a lifetime next year, we will have more children, we will both work like stink and then take early retirement, she/he runs domestic affairs entirely, and she/he will always be main breadwinner. These expectations may be need to be reviewed and revised in the light of big change.

Other expectations of your relationship with your partner may be to do with how your relationship works. You may have to ask yourself:

Am I trying to manager her/him and our relationship too much?

Some of us have problems being clear about the boundaries between ourselves and our partners. So if our partner is demotivated for whatever reason, we will believe that we can control them and get them to make changes. This is unrealistic; the most we can expect to do is to inspire them to change their attitudes and behaviour.

We may need to ask ourselves, too, if the changes we are so keen to make in our partner are changes that we would like to see in ourselves.

Am I trying to be right in helping them, rather than encouraging what makes us both happy?

When situations are confusing, we often become very concerned about doing the 'right' thing. So if your partner's recovering from a professional or health setback, you may read books and articles, rather like this one, that tell you to 'cure stress by taking exercise several times a week'. You dutifully get up every morning and nag your partner into doing some exercise. They do it resentfully, vowing that they'll quit as soon as you're off their back. Your partner may actually not feel well enough to do exercise at this particular time, and you might be wiser either saying that you're going to the gym yourself and they can have a lift, or suggesting that they might like to join you for an afternoon stroll a bit later. Key words here are, 'I was wondering whether you might like to . . .' rather than 'You really should' or 'You must . . .'. If they make the choice to take action, they are much more likely to continue to be motivated to do so.

Am I stuck in a pattern of blaming my partner and thinking that they owe me for services?

Big changes in anyone's life has ramifications for those who live with them. We may feel angry, guilty and frustrated at our situation, and blame our partner for these feelings. We may feel very put-upon, in that we may find ourselves rushing around performing much of our partner's role in the family as well as our own. It's healthy and sensible to acknowledge these feelings – not necessarily to our partner at the time, but to ourselves – and then to give ourselves some sort of compensation. In my view, these take the form of Galaxy bars, lipsticks, magazines, unsuitably fashionable and cheap items of clothing, and walks on the beach.

There is undoubtedly a transactional element to most relationships: you give him optimism, he gives you stability; you give him intimate caring, he gives you great sex; you organise a great social life for him, and he gives you a certain social standing. But if every aspect of your relationship becomes transactional, you are reducing it to the level of shopkeeper and supplier. There will be no place for emotional connections, for building on the feelings that originally attracted you to one another, and for strengthening them as you encounter life's uncertainties together. While competitiveness can have a role in a relationship, mutual support should be a higher priority.

Is too much of my self-esteem invested in my partner?

Your identity is separate from that of your partner. Ideally, the main thing that you have in common is your mutual concern for one another's well-being. You will be more helpful to your partner if you *don't* join them in feeling exactly the same way that they do; rather, hold back a bit so that you can see what they need more of.

'But enough thinking about my attitudes,' I hear you cry. 'What can I *do* to help them?'. Here goes, then:

Become their biggest fan

Praise your partner very specifically; really show appreciation to them and boost their sense of self-worth whenever you can. Just to repeat my earlier advice, when we deal with crisis management: save half an hour a day to worry about what their change in circumstances means to you and the family.

Handle disagreements wisely

When your partner's spoiling for a fight out of frustration, or you are genuinely in disagreement over something, choose to disagree over the *issue* rather than the relationship. Remember that you are emotionally connected and love each other. Your emotional connection and long-term relationship is ultimately much bigger than any single issue about which you might disagree. Draw this to get a better perspective if it helps.

Resolve to enjoy the present

As your long-term plans may have had to be put on hold, resolve to enjoy the present, through the small but highly significant things in life. Prepare and eat really healthy food, look after yourself and present yourself as best you can, and live each day with as much love and fun as you can.

Bolster even when criticising

If your partner's behaviour is becoming self-abusive, or threatens the family health, you obviously need to point this out. But pointing it out in the context of what you consider to be their overriding virtues is the best way of doing this. Something along the lines of: 'I'm objecting to this behaviour and you are such a considerate person usually' is normally most effective.

When someone is demotivated for a long period of time, it can be difficult to assess the extent to which the relationship has been affected by your partner's behaviour. You could ask yourself:

Do we still have some of the emotional connections we had when we first met?

You might want to remind your partner of these connections, by reminiscing about the good times when you first got together, and the highlights, since. A break away somewhere, even if it is just for a weekend, could be a good opportunity to revive these feelings.

Inspiring a demotivated child

Although parents hold a great deal of responsibility for their children, we are certainly not *totally* responsible for phases they go through and the adults they become. Other forces, such as their peers, the environment they frequent, their hormones and their own very distinctive individual biology will play a part. too. As they grow to adulthood, we cannot be completely responsible for who they are. David, a lawyer, has the following view:

While my kids were growing up we really tried hard to create an environment in which they felt safe and loved, were allowed to express themselves pretty freely and were encouraged to develop a good moral sense. In their teens, though, they rebelled and I just couldn't understand it. It was really hurtful; all our efforts seemed to be for nothing. We had to resign ourselves to accept that no matter how great our efforts, they were going to be rebellious teenagers, and we were powerless in the face of raging hormones and peer-group pressure.

Emotional rescue

In his book, *Emotional Intelligence*, Daniel Goleman argues a powerful case for 'self-science' to be taught in the school curriculum. This would cover subjects like self-awareness, decision-making, self-esteem, personal strengths and weaknesses, conflict handling, and positive but not un-realistic thinking. He cites instances of similar programmes effectively halving mild depression and relationship diffi-culties in a group of ten to thirteen-year-olds, with this reduction being maintained for at least two years. In another example, he describes a programme for unpopular children, where they acted as consultants to a coach who wanted to learn all about the kinds of things that children did to make it more enjoyable to play games. Again there was an over 50 percent improvement in popularity with the children, though I'm not sure exactly how you would measure this . . .

Certainly our formal, traditional education system has ignored emotional influences on motivation and how children learn. Yet, if you're like me, and many of the people I know, when we recollect our schooldays it is always the teacher we *liked* best who we remember and who seems to have had the most profound influence on us.

I have especially vivid memories of this; until the age of about fourteen, and for some bizarre reason, I excelled at chemistry. I still have a school report that says, 'Chemistry 100 percent; outstanding and brilliant'. The master told my parents that I was the most exceptional student he had ever encountered. That was until the day Form 4F arrived early in the chemistry lab, and I decided to dismantle Dr Stokes' elaborate model of the atom, entertaining the rest of 4F to a cabaret of sputniks and dogs made from its component parts. To say Dr Stokes went ballistic would be an understatement. I was relegated to the back of the lab and given a thousand lines to write out. On the next exam I got 40 percent, and my chemical aspirations never raised their fizzy vapours again. And all because of a teacher's reaction.

Ins and outs

In our affluent, hugely materialistic society we are surrounded by encouragement to motivate ourselves and our kids through external rewards. And I'm as guilty as the next woman of motivating myself through spending most of my publishing advance on expensive clothes I don't need before I've started the book, or getting half an hour to read the papers by bribing my four and six-year-olds into peace through the reward of a new Thunderbirds video at the weekend. But external rewards have to get bigger and more frequent if they are to work as motivators, and eventually the bank manager calls, or the credit card gets turned down at the till in the video store. Finances apart, do we want to raise kids with a very limited view of what rewards matter in life? That is, do we want their motivation to be purely monetary and materialistic?

Parents are certainly in a difficult position today, and there is no doubt that the likes of Disney and McDonald's seem to have a conspiracy afoot, to ensure that we motivate our little darlings through the latest craze they have on offer. However much short-term docility we inspire through the 'do it and I'll buy it' approach to parenting, we ultimately gain nothing in the long term, and that's what needs to be addressed. We need to resolve to help our children understand their own reactions and responses to what they want a bit better, and in doing so, we can give them a lifelong means of motivating themselves. The key to this is:

Empathy

In these times of government-led initiatives on 'emotional literacy', empathy has become a rather trendy word. But what exactly does it mean? Well, unlike sympathy, it's not about feeling sorry for people. Rather, it's an appreciation of feelings, and an attempt to understand others, without necessarily experiencing those feelings ourselves.

Empathy between parent and child is the most powerful means of helping children to learn to motivate themselves, because our children start to see us as friends and allies. Developing it with our children involves:

Noticing the emotion. Very often, of course, we can't help doing this, especially as the expression of emotion usually comes at inconvenient times. Just when we're about to put a load through the till at the supermarket, for instance, or about to leave to go on a critical business trip. At times like this, it can be very easy to dismiss the emotion with a 'Don't be silly', or challenging it with a 'Don't you dare do that'. And yes, we need to be aware of messages we received as children about the expression of emotions that may influence our responses here. Take Lynne, for example:

> *I grew up with a very volatile father, who had unpredictable bouts of anger. He was an emotional tyrant, his own needs being the only ones that mattered in our family. As a result, the rest of us only expressed our emotions in private, and it's left me with a dread of anyone getting angry. I very, very rarely express anger myself and when I see it in other*

people, I immediately try to mollify them. When my toddler started to have bouts of anger, I was struck by panic. Was he inheriting his grandfather's volatility? Shouldn't I do everything in my power to calm him, immediately? These angry bouts became more frequent and I became increasingly desperate trying to pacify him. Then a good friend, who is also a mum, suggested a different tack. She said to let my little boy stay angry for a while, observe his state rather than rushing in to pacify him immediately, and then to try and talk to him about it. She gave me that rather radical idea that 'Maybe him getting angry isn't your fault'. It's hard to rework conditioning like this, but I think I've almost succeeded in viewing his emotions as a way of improving the way we communicate together, rather than something I'm terrified of.

Validating the emotion. This means letting children know that it is OK to express whatever it is they are feeling. Validation needs to be considered alongside the often helpful idea that one way of coping with unwelcome emotion is to distract ourselves. Hence the popularity of absorbing books, films and copious amounts of alcohol for nervous flyers. But if we use distraction too often and too quickly as a means of helping our children to cope with emotion, they may conclude that emotional expression in itself is a bad thing. And speaking as a mum rather than any sort of child development expert, I'd say that age is certainly relevant here. Babies and very small children often benefit greatly from soothing distraction. At around about three or four though, children seem to start to be able to use verbal expression about their feelings.

As they get older, it's helpful for them to know that

while any sort of emotional expression to you is valid, the same guideline does not go for behaviour. Your seven-year-old may feel and express deep hatred for her four-year-old sibling, but actually inflicting bodily harm is another thing altogether.

Help label the emotion. What you're doing here is giving your child a vocabulary of emotions. And this involves spending time in conversation, no matter how difficult it is to drag them away from the video or computer screen. It helps them to understand that fury at somebody else winning something is called jealousy, that sadness for the deceased absent grandparent is called longing, and that really looking forward to something turning out well is called hope. This is emotional literacy, and when we are equipped with it, it helps us to understand our own complex feelings and those of other people.

Problem solving and setting limits. When our children are able to tell us how they feel, we can then clarify with them the problem that is causing these feelings. And then we can move on to what they would like to do to handle this problem. Often when they are small we may need to make lots of suggestions here: accepting the loss of a grand-parent may be eased by thinking about the lovely times they spent together; fury at a younger sibling's inability to share toys may be eased by setting periods of time when the toys can be used. The more children generate their own solutions to these problems, the better for their emotional intelligence as adults.

Problem-solving in this way is, ultimately, goal-setting. In the same way that it works in sport, at work and in adult personal development, we need to give lots of acknowl-edgement to the goal being reached and lots of consideration to how our children will feel then.

Different types of parenting

Researcher Diana Baimriol identified three different types of parenting and their effects on children's development. The first type is an authoritarian style: as we might expect, it is characterised by many rules being set, an emphasis on unquestioning obedience and no exploration of emotions, wants and needs. This tends to result in children growing into adults who often experience conflict inside and who tend to be irritable fairly frequently.

In contrast, the second type is a permissive style, where parents are warm and communicative, but set virtually no rules or boundaries. Their style might be based on 'child-centred' ideas, but to the extent that it is highly indulgent. Rather surprisingly to some of the more ardent champions of this approach, children reared this way tend to be impulsive, aggressive, low in self-reliance and low in achievement.

The third type is described as an authoritative style. This involves setting rules and boundaries with a fair amount of flexibility; these behaviours are accompanied by lots of explanation and warmth towards the children. You won't be surprised to hear that this style tends to create adults who are consistently co-operative, self-reliant, energetic, friendly and achievement-oriented.

The effects of these different styles are hardly surprising. When discipline is too strong and inhibiting, there is bound to be internal conflict and confusion about emotions that are taboo. When the parenting style is over-indulgent, children miss out on learning respect and also fail to learn to self-regulate. Relationships can be difficult for them: because they haven't learnt the self-control that makes us attractive to one another, and the ability to compromise when we make friends and lovers. When the style is a half-way house between two of these, children learn to acknowledge and handle their emotions, and to negotiate with far greater skill the balance between their own needs and those of other people. In short, they live much happier lives.

Emotional coaching

We can be quite creative in helping children identify and handle their emotions. Drawing and painting how they feel about things can be helpful, as can acting out scenes with toys. Different scenarios can be drawn or acted out as alternative possible goals.

Sometimes, it can be helpful to investigate children's fantasies about how things would be if they got what they really wanted in a situation. They then need to work back from this to a goal that is realistic, with boundaries that consider reality and the responses of others involved.

As often as possible, it helps to use characters and situations with which children really identify. In our house at the moment, when our sons start to argue, I am enjoying success – probably brief, until the next trend comes along – with a problem-solving exercise about what their Thunderbird heroes, the Tracy brothers, would do in such a situation. At least, they're more moral than Pokémon.

And what about our own emotions?

Laura is a mother of five-year-old twins:

> Sometimes I feel as a parent that I'm not meant to have any feelings of my own, that they must be completely subsumed in order to serve and develop my children. I get really frustrated and pent-up, so that by the time they go to bed, I'm just desperate for a drink and a huge emotional blow-out. And, yes, it's my partner who bears the brunt of this.

This approach, with its emphasis on helping children to self-regulate, means that it's OK for parents to express their own emotions in front of their children; however, the idea is that it's much more helpful to direct emotions like anger at a specific problem rather than a child's personality or character. So a global condemnation, of the 'You are a complete brat' variety, is out; however, specific description of behaviour and effect, such as 'You are making me mad through that horrible noise' is in.

Finally . . . friends

I'm sure your common sense will tell you that many of the guidelines I've given for motivating partners and children also work with friends. In friendship, however, the transactional nature of the relationship, the 'You scratch my back then I'll scratch yours' scenario, often matters more. It's a great act of friendship to help a chum remotivate themselves after a divorce, bereavement or redundancy, but if your friendship turns permanently to that of counsellor and client, you may need to have a frank conversation about this.

Chatting about how your friendship has developed over the years, and the respective roles you've both played in it, can be useful, with a clear indication of how you would look forward to support and encouragement in the future, were you to need it. When someone's leaning on you too much, seeing them less and changing where you meet and what you do together can also help shift the balance.

And you

This book has covered motivating ourselves and others from many different angles and in many different contexts. I would like to remind you now that we live in a wonderful laboratory known as 'real life'. Choose what is useful to you from these chapters and go out and experiment. And may you discover unexpected delights as a result.

When I'm demotivated during writing, I remind myself that I regard you readers as unknown friends: people with whom I would easily connect were I to meet you. My known friends rarely ask me for advice; they either doubt my wisdom or are sensitive to my feelings of working overtime. When they do ask me, I have one philosophy. Forget control, order and the illusion that you can minimise uncertainty; live most days like they are rationed. Fill your life with interests, whether they are reflective or action-packed. Leap in and try to experience as much as you can. Make decisions based on experience, rather than fear of the future. That is how you will get up and grow to fulfilment. Your goal is exuberance. Viva!

Recommended Reading

de Bono, Edward: *Serious Creativity* (HarperCollins, 1996)
Davies, Philippa: *Irresistibility – Secrets of Selling Yourself* (Coronet, 2001)
Davies, Philippa: *Total Confidence* (Piatkus, 1994)
Davies, Philippa: *Your Total Image* (Piatkus, 1990)
Gottman, John: *The Heart of Parenting* (Bloomsbury, 1997)
Kubler-Ross, Elisabeth: *On Death and Dying* (Routledge, 1973)
Thayer, Robert. E: *The Origin of Everyday Moods* (Oxford, 1996)
Storr, Anthony: *The School of Genius* (Andre Deutsch, 1988)

Career Counselling

Career Counselling Services, 46 Ferry Road, London SW13 9PW
020 8741-0335 www.career-counselling-services.co.uk

For details of getupandgrow, Philippa Davies' company please contact:
www.getupandgrow.co.uk or phone 02920 705723 or fax 02920 705724